Poka-yoke

Improving Product Quality by Preventing Defects

Poka-yoke
Improving Product Quality by Preventing Defects

Edited by
Nikkan Kogyo Shimbun, Ltd./Factory Magazine

With an overview by
Hiroyuki Hirano
Chairman of the Board,
JIT Management Laboratory Company, Ltd.

Publisher's Foreword by
Norman Bodek
President, Productivity, Inc.

Productivity Press
Cambridge, Massachusetts / Norwalk, Connecticut

Originally published as *Pokayoke dai zukan*, copyright © 1987 by The Nikkan Kogyo Shimbun, Ltd., Tokyo.

English translation copyright © 1988 by Productivity Press, Inc.

Productivity Press
P.O. Box 3007
Cambridge MA 02140
(617) 497-5146

or

Productivity, Inc.
101 Merritt 7 Corporate Park
5th Floor
Norwalk CT 06851
(203) 846-3777

Cover design by Gail Graves
Book design by Susan Cobb
Set in Berling by Rudra Press, Cambridge MA
Printed and bound by The Maple-Vail Book Manufacturing Group
Printed in the United States of America

Library of Congress Catalog Card Number: 88-62593
ISBN: 0-915299-31-3

Library of Congress Cataloging-in-Publication Data

Pokayoke dai zukan.   English.
  Poka-yoke.

  Translation of: Pokayoke dai zukan.
  Includes index.
  1. Quality control.   I. Nikkan kōgyō shimbun.
II. Title.
TS156.P6413   1988   658.5'6   88-62593
ISBN: 0-915299-31-3

91 10 9 8 7 6 5 4

Contents

Publisher's Foreword

"What's the secret? It's a mystery to me — our plant is as sophisticated as you can get, yet with all this innovation at our disposal we still make defects. I can't believe all those statistics about parts per million and zero defects coming from Japan. There must be a gimmick. With all the variability of parts coming from hundreds of vendors and going through fifty different processes with a hundred machines, it is impossible not to produce some defects. So what's the trick? Where is the hidden weapon?"

You too may be a little confused and frustrated with the concept of zero defects and by now tired and disbelieving of all the stories about quality and Japanese manufacturing productivity.

Our company leads study missions that take manufacturing people through Japanese plants to learn about these methods that have helped reshape the international economic order. I want you to know that in our visits to over 200 different Japanese plants these past ten years, we have seen with our own eyes the quality charts and the multitude of simple poka-yoke devices used to prevent defects from occurring. It is not *one* device, but the application of hundreds and thousands of these very simple "fail-safing" mechanisms that day after day has brought the quality miracle to Japan. Each one is relatively simple — something you easily could do on your own. It is the totality, the hundreds of devices, that is almost frightening to behold.

On one line producing washing machines we saw over 300 small devices, each designed to either stop the line before a defect occurred or signal an operator to come quickly to examine a potential problem.

I saw many sensors lined up to inspect 100 percent of the work. Every single operation was checked before it moved on. These checks normally detected errors before a defect could occur. And many of the devices were thought up and installed by the workers themselves.

Since we know you will continue to be skeptical unless you see it for yourself, we dedicate this book to you, the American manufacturer — line workers and supervisors as well as management — and recommend that you review each picture, each example, to see for yourself how these simple devices can absolutely prevent defects.

We are indebted to Dr. Shigeo Shingo for perfecting the methodology of poka-yoke and to the numerous factory managers and workers that submitted their ideas to Nikkan Kogyo Shimbun for publication.

The concept of poka-yoke is much too significant to limit to an engineering or design department removed from the daily experience of the manufacturing floor. We hope that this book will be seriously studied and used diligently in study groups by line workers and supervisors. It was designed with the intent to involve employees, at every level, in the process of eliminating all defects from production. We hope that American industry will use these ideas widely and quickly to help bring their companies to world class status.

I would like to thank Karen Jones and Nils Davis for their editorial work on *Poka-yoke*, and Rosemary Winfield for copyediting; Karen Jones for the indexes; and Esmé McTighe and Gail Graves for production. The cover was designed by Gail Graves. The interior was designed by Susan Cobb and composed by Michele Seery and Caroline Kutil of Rudra Press, Cambridge, Massachusetts.

Norman Bodek
President
Productivity, Inc.

Preface

There are three major inspection techniques in the field of quality control:

1. *Judgment inspection* — Separates defective products from good ones after processing. It prevents defects from being delivered to customers, but does not decrease a company's defect rate.
2. *Informative inspection* — Investigates the causes of defects and feeds back this information to the appropriate processes so that action can be taken to reduce the defect rate.
3. *Source inspection* — A defect is a result, or an *effect*, usually caused by a simple mistake. Through 100 percent inspection at the source, the mistake can be corrected before it becomes a defect. "Defects = Zero" can be achieved.

Statistical process control (SPC) developed in the United States. SPC activities are based on the premise that 100 percent inspection is burdensome and time-consuming and can be adequately replaced by sampling inspection and statistics. But statistics is really no more than qualified guesswork. Because there is always some discrepancy with the reality, a certain level of defects is tolerated. In a Zero Quality Control (ZQC) system, however, 100 percent inspection is achieved through poka-yoke, an approach that is inexpensive and requires little effort.

Informative inspection sounds effective, but because the check-feedback-action cycle does not begin until after defects occur, it essentially tolerates their existence. SPC is merely a tool of quality *control*; it cannot eliminate the source of defects. It is said that there is no quality control without control charts, but control charts only help maintain the accepted defect rate — they cannot reduce defects to zero.

Zero Quality Control has three components that lead to the elimination of defects:

1. *Source inspection* — Checks for factors that cause errors, not the resulting defect.
2. *100 percent inspection* — Uses inexpensive poka-yoke (mistake-proofing) devices to inspect automatically for errors or defective operating conditions.
3. *Immediate action* — Operations are stopped instantly when a mistake is made and not resumed until it is corrected.

Together, these are the key elements of "Zero Quality Control," a system that can lead to "Defects = Zero" when applied with care.* Poka-yoke devices in particular play a major role in ZQC as tools for 100 percent inspection. The examples in this book show simple, inexpensive techniques for eliminating or at least reducing defects and the mistakes that cause them. As the inventor of poka-yoke, I will be very pleased to see these ideas implemented in U.S. factories as tools to achieve zero defects. I would like to conclude by emphasizing once again that poka-yoke must be clearly understood as a tool to achieve Zero Quality Control.

The three features of zero quality control can be weighted in importance as follows:

Source inspection:	*60 percent*
100 percent inspection (poka-yoke):	*30 percent*
Immediate action:	*10 percent*

As you can see, source inspection is the most important function, with 100 percent inspection, using poka-yoke, as a tool for achieving it. Please keep this priority of function in mind as you review the actual cases presented in this book and apply them in your own workplace.

Shigeo Shingo

---

* See Shigeo Shingo, *Zero Quality Control: Source Inspection and the Poka-yoke System*, Cambridge, MA: Productivity Press, 1986. This definitive work on poka-yoke is available from Productivity Press, P.O Box 3007, Cambridge MA 02140, (617) 497-5146.

Introduction

Not so long ago a small English dictionary was published for Japanese school-children to use in studying for their exams. To encourage their efforts, it came with a little printed bookmark that read "A person is an animal that forgets. Learn more than you forget!"

The fact is, human beings are very forgetful and tend to make mistakes. Too often we blame people for making mistakes. Especially in the workplace, this attitude not only discourages workers and lowers morale, but it does not solve the problem. *Poka-yoke* is a technique for avoiding simple human error at work.

What Is Poka-yoke?

Although the concept of poka-yoke has existed for a long time in various forms, it was Japanese manufacturing engineer Shigeo Shingo who developed the idea into a formidable tool for achieving zero defects and eventually *eliminating* quality control inspections.* The methods he advocates were formerly called "fool-proofing." Recognizing that this label could offend many workers, Shingo came up with the term poka-yoke, generally translated as "mistake-proofing" or "fail-safing" (to avoid (*yokeru*) inadvertent errors (*poka*)). The idea behind poka-yoke is to respect the intelligence of workers. By taking over repetitive tasks or actions that depend on vigilance or memory, poka-yoke can free a worker's time and mind to pursue more creative and value-adding activities.

Many things can go wrong in the complex environment of the workplace; every day there are opportunities to make mistakes that will result in defective products. Defects are wasteful, and if they are not discovered, they disappoint the customer's expectations of quality. Behind poka-yoke is the conviction that it is not acceptable to produce even a small number of defective goods. To become a world-class competitor, a company must adopt not only a philosophy but a *practice* of producing zero defects. Poka-yoke methods are simple concepts for achieving this goal.

Types of Poka-yoke Devices

In this book, poka-yoke is used in a broad sense to describe worker-originated improvements that incorporate one or more of the main components of Shingo's Zero Quality Control system:

1. Source inspection to detect errors at their source — before they cause defects. An example is an additional locator pin to prevent misalignment of the workpiece.
2. 100% inspection for defects using an inexpensive sensing device such as a limit switch.
3. Immediate action to stop operations when an error is detected, such as an interlocked circuit that automatically shuts down the machine.

Of course, the first technique — preventing the defect in the first place — is the most effective, but devices for catching defects and immediately stopping the action are also valuable parts of the defect reduction process. Applications of many of these devices are shown in the following pages; see Dr. Shingo's book, *Zero Quality Control: Source Inspection and the Poka-yoke System* for descriptions of the devices themselves.

The examples also include improvements that properly could be called design changes — alterations that go beyond machine and process improvements to affect the shape of the product itself. Many of these are extremely simple, such as eliminating unused holes in a circuit board to avoid errors in inserting a plug. In many companies, however, the design function traditionally has been carried out almost exclusively by engineering or design. Although these departments generally take manufacturing factors into consideration, products today often go through several stages of refinement and redesign. In keeping with the spirit of poka-yoke, the design refinement process should incorporate the experiences of the production workers, since they are in the best position to discover design elements that cause difficulty but serve no value-adding function.

You don't need a highly automated factory to take advantage of the ideas here. These devices can be as simple and inexpensive as an interference pin for a jig or a limit switch to signal correct placement of the workpiece. Nor do the devices make an employee's skill unnecessary. Some, like the color-coded wiring template, simply assist the worker in performing a task correctly. Others, such as a counter, or an alarm to signal a defect, require a worker to take some responsive action. Strictly speaking, these latter innovations are not entirely mistake-proof, since to be effective they depend on the worker to voluntarily respond appropriately. When employees are motivated and interested in improving the product or process, however, such helpful devices can significantly reduce the number of mistakes and are therefore included here.

The responsibility for a successful "Zero Defects" campaign ultimately rests on management. The leaders of the company must themselves have a vision of the quality the company can produce, and must create a company culture and environment that motivates employees throughout the company to make that vision their own. This may mean providing time and support resources for work teams to analyze problems. It may mean instituting an incentive-based suggestion system to encourage workers to solve the problems that cause defects.** At the most basic level, it means recognizing the inherent expertise of the people who are doing the work and creating channels through which they can express this knowledge, and above all, maintaining an atmosphere in which they will *want* to express it for the benefit of the company.

About This Book

Operators in more than 100 Japanese plants created and implemented the 240 poka-yoke improvement examples in this book, which was compiled by the staff of Nikkan Kogyo Shimbun, Ltd. from a series that originally appeared in *Factory* magazine. Many industries are represented here, including companies that produce some of the world's best-selling audio products, automotive components, computers, cameras, and apparel. The first section of the book, presented in the cartoon style used in Japan for serious topics as well as comics, summarizes many of the concepts or main features of poka-yoke.

The examples are organized according to the broad issue or problem they address. In addition to these classifications, several finding aids are provided. The index of devices and methods pinpoints examples using specific poka-yoke devices. The index of operations and problems and index of parts and products help you find ideas that have eliminated defects in a particular type of work or product.

Whether you are a worker, a supervisor, an engineer, or a manager, these examples should spark your imagination in planning and implementing mistake-preventing systems in your work environment. We hope you — individuals as well as study groups — will actively discuss, use, copy, adapt, multiply, and improve on the ideas compiled here. We have provided blank improvement forms following the examples for you to sketch out your own ideas.

"A person is an animal that makes mistakes. Therefore we must practice poka-yoke more than we make errors."

---

* For more about the history and elements of the Zero Quality Control system, see Shigeo Shingo, *Zero Quality Control: Source Inspection and the Poka-yoke System*, Cambridge, MA: Productivity Press, 1986. Available from Productivity Press, P.O. Box 3007, Cambridge MA 02140, (617) 497-5146.

** For guidance in developing a living suggestion system that will encourage your employees' creative involvement in preventing defects as well as in cost reduction and other goals, see *The Idea Book: Improvement Through TEI (Total Employee Involvement)*, Cambridge, MA: Productivity Press, 1988. This is the only English-language handbook on the "continuous improvement" suggestion system *(teian)*, widely used in Japanese companies not only to improve competitive position by generating and implementing a large number of ideas, but to build a strong, participative environment that respects the intelligence and creativity of the workers. Available from Productivity Press, P.O. Box 3007, Cambridge, MA 02140, (617) 497-5146.

Poka-yoke

Improving Product Quality by Preventing Defects

Overview of Poka-yoke
by Hiroyuki Hirano
JIT Management Laboratory Company, Ltd.

A Successful Modern Factory

"Inadvertent mistakes increase work."

To survive in the competitive atmosphere of modern manufacturing, a company must adhere strictly to standards. While customers must be satisfied with all aspects of products and service, the company must still make a profit and protect its workers. In a successful modern factory:

Sales price = market price
Sell at a price consumers are willing to pay.

Diversity = many kinds of products in small numbers
Make only what consumers need.

Quality = highest possible quality
Make products that will satisfy consumers.

Delivery = always on time
Always meet delivery schedules. Deliver products just when consumers need them.

Cost = lowest unit cost
Produce at the lowest possible cost while satisfying consumer requirements.

Safety = always first
Turn out safe products safely.

Do You Have a Consumer-driven Company?

A manufacturer that makes products to satisfy consumers is "consumer driven" or "outside-in." On the other hand, a factory that makes products that are forced on consumers is "producer driven" or "inside-out." In today's competitive economy, a company must be consumer driven to be successful. How are things in *your* factory?

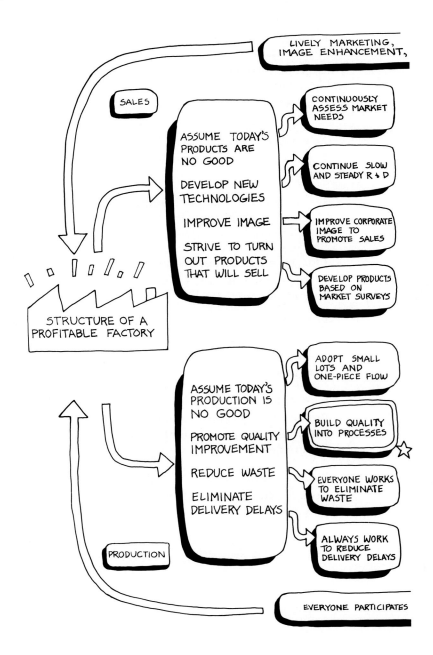

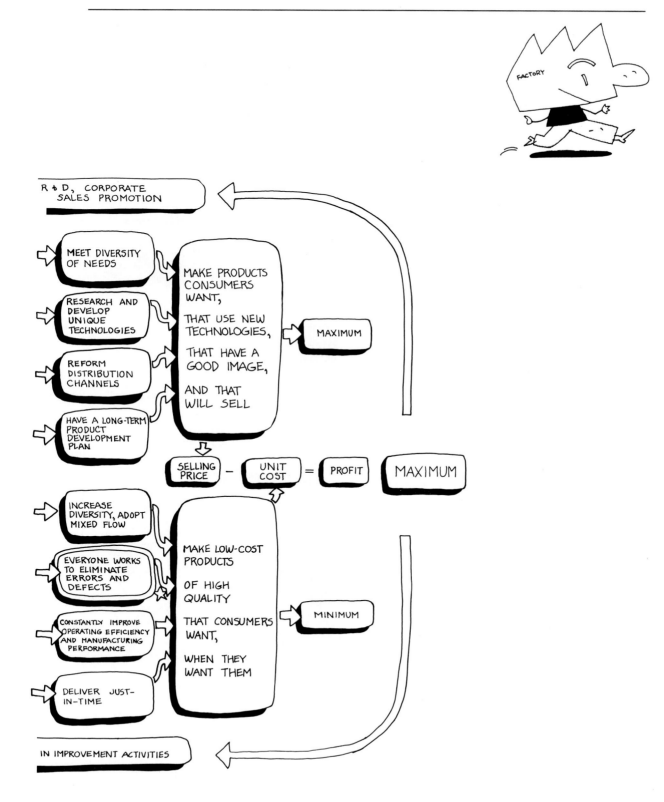

All About Defects

Are Errors Unavoidable?

There are two approaches to dealing with errors:

• **Errors are inevitable!**

People always make mistakes. While we tend to accept the mistakes as natural, we blame the people who make them. With this kind of attitude, we're likely to overlook defects as they occur in production. They may be detected only in final inspection or, worse yet, by the customer.

• **Errors can be eliminated!**

Any kind of mistake people make can be reduced or even eliminated. People make fewer mistakes if they are supported by proper training and by a production system based on the principle that errors can always be prevented.

Is Sampling Inspection Really the Best Method?

One method of preventing errors is inspection. There are two major types of inspection.

• Sampling inspection

Some plant managers say, "It would take us all day to inspect all our products. There may be a few defects, but sampling is still the most practical way to check. We maintain our quality at an average quality level (AQL) of 0.1 percent."

But this means that one consumer in a thousand will get a defective product! For that consumer, the product is 100 percent defective, not 0.1 percent defective. Sampling inspection makes sense only from the manufacturer's view, not from the consumer's.

• 100 percent inspection makes the most sense!

In the best factories, the attitude is, "We won't tolerate a single defect! We'll organize production so that 100 percent of the products can be inspected easily. That makes the most sense!"

Today, even one defective product is enough to destroy a consumer's confidence in the company. To stay competitive, a company must supply good products in the tens and hundreds of thousands. The best way to achieve this is to organize production to inspect 100 percent of the products.

The User Is the Best Inspector

No one intends to make mistakes. But while we are working, defects can show up without our noticing. We usually think we're doing the job right, even as we mistakenly mount the wrong part or drill a hole in the wrong position. How can we catch these errors before they turn into defective products?

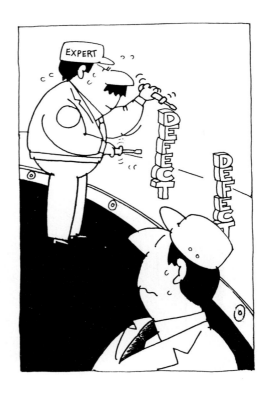

• Finding defects in the subsequent process

We don't expect to find defects, but if a product we use doesn't do what it is supposed to do, we know it's defective. Users are the best at discovering defects.

Since subsequent processes are also "users" of the product being manufactured, they are also expert at finding defects. If products are produced in a continuous flow, each product or part is sent to the next process as soon as it is finished, and defects are therefore found immediately.

Three Strategies for Zero Defects

1. Don't make it!

Don't make products you don't need. The more products you make, the greater the opportunity for defects as they sit in inventory. Therefore, follow the *just-in-time* principle and make only what is needed, when it is needed, and in the amount needed. Scratches and nicks will decrease dramatically.

2. Make it to withstand any use!

The user is an expert at finding defects. Therefore it is important to build safeguards into the production process to ensure that the product can withstand any use. Quality can be built into products by thoroughly implementing *poka-yoke*, *automation*, and *work standardization*.

3. Once you've made it, use it right away!

If a product cannot be made to withstand any use, then make sure it is used as soon as possible by using *continuous flow production*.

There Are Different Kinds of Errors

Almost all defects are caused by human errors. However, there are at least ten kinds of human errors.

1. *Forgetfulness:* Sometimes we forget things when we are not concentrating. For example, the stationmaster forgets to lower the crossing gate. *Safeguards:* Alerting operator in advance or checking at regular intervals.

2. *Errors due to misunderstanding:* Sometimes we make mistakes when we jump to the wrong conclusion before we're familiar with the situation. For example, a person not used to a car with automatic transmission steps on the brake, thinking it is the clutch. *Safeguards:* Training, checking in advance, standardizing work procedures.

3. *Errors in identification:* Sometimes we misjudge a situation because we view it too quickly or are too far away to see it clearly. For example, a $1 bill is mistaken for a $10 bill. *Safeguards:* Training, attentiveness, vigilance.

4. *Errors made by amateurs:* Sometimes we make mistakes through lack of experience. For example, a new worker does not know the operation or is just barely familiar with it. *Safeguards:* Skill building, work standardization.

5. *Willful errors:* Sometimes errors occur when we decide that we can ignore rules under certain circumstances. For example, crossing a street against a red light because there are no cars in sight at the moment. *Safeguards:* Basic education and experience.

6. *Inadvertent errors:* Sometimes we are absentminded and make mistakes without knowing how they happened. For example, someone lost in thought tries to cross the street without even noticing that the light is red. *Safeguards:* Attentiveness, discipline, work standardization.

7. *Errors due to slowness:* Sometimes we make mistakes when our actions are slowed down by delays in judgment. For example, a person learning to drive is slow to step on the brake. *Safeguards:* Skill building, work standardization.

8. *Errors due to lack of standards:* Some errors occur when there are no suitable instructions or work standards. For example, a measurement may be left to an individual worker's discretion. *Safeguards:* Work standardization, work instructions.

9. *Surprise errors:* Errors sometimes occur when equipment runs differently than expected. For example, a machine might malfunction without warning. *Safeguards:* Total productive maintenance, work standardization.

10. *Intentional errors:* Some people make mistakes deliberately. Crimes and sabotage are examples. *Safeguards:* Fundamental education, discipline.

Mistakes happen for many reasons, but almost all can be prevented if we take the time to identify when and why they happen and then take steps to prevent them by using poka-yoke methods and the safeguards listed above.

There Are Different Kinds of Defects, Too

What kinds of defects are caused by human errors?

- *Example:* Cut surfaces are covered with burrs.
  Cause: Someone did not replace the cutting tools on time.
- *Example:* Machinery malfunctions, resulting in defects.
  Cause: Regular inspection of the machinery has been neglected.
- *Example:* Processing mistakes resulted in defects.
  Cause: Someone mistook a workpiece of one type for one of another type.

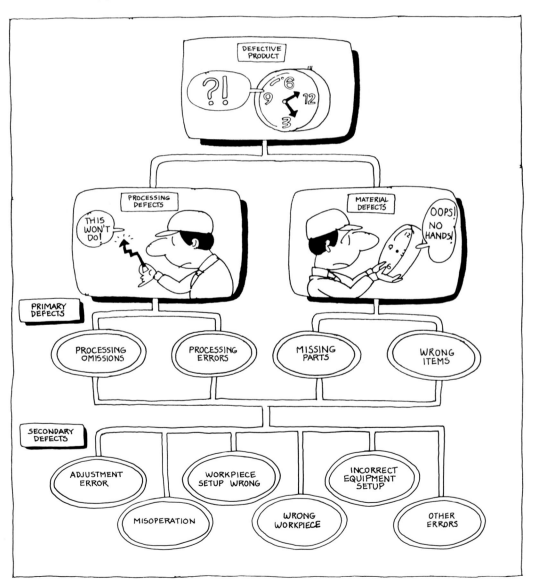

The Five Elements of Production

Everyday work in the manufacturing plant is aimed at turning out products consumers will like. Break down daily activities in a factory and you will find that: In response to work instructions (*Information*), parts and materials (*Material*) are obtained and set up on machinery and equipment (*Machinery*), where workers (*Me*) make things in accordance with the established standard operating procedure (*Method*).

These five elements (4M and 1I) determine whether a product is correctly manufactured or a defect is made. Defect-free products are assured by controls in each of these areas.

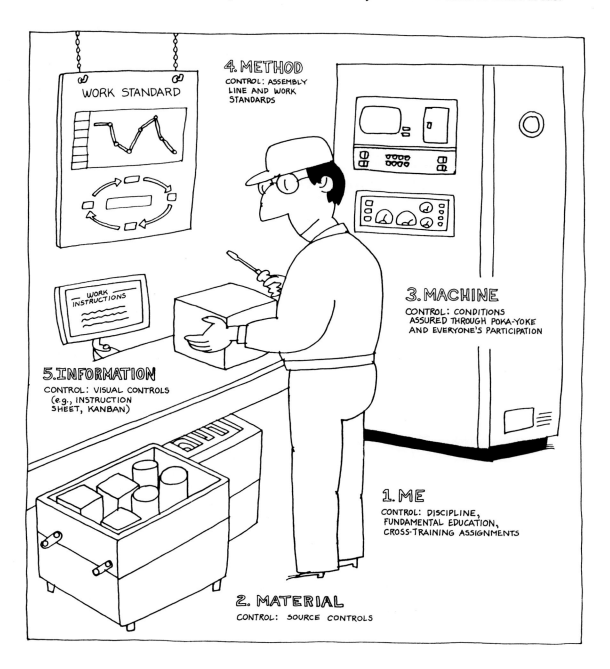

What Are the Sources of Defects?

There are various types of defects. In order of importance these are:

1. Omitted processing
2. Processing errors
3. Errors setting up workpieces
4. Missing parts
5. Wrong parts
6. Processing wrong workpiece
7. Misoperation
8. Adjustment error
9. Equipment not set up properly
10. Tools and jigs improperly prepared

What are the connections between these defects and the mistakes people make?

☆ CAUSAL CONNECTIONS BETWEEN DEFECTS AND HUMAN ERRORS

◉ STRONGLY CONNECTED   ○ CONNECTED

CAUSES OF DEFECTS \ HUMAN ERRORS	INTENTIONAL	MISUNDERSTANDING	FORGETFUL	MISIDENTIFICATION	AMATEURS	WILLFUL	INADVERTENT	SLOWNESS	NON-SUPERVISION	SURPRISE
OMITTED PROCESSING	◉	○	◉	○	○	○	◉	○	○	
PROCESSING ERRORS	◉	◉	○	○	◉	◉	◉	◉	◉	
ERRORS SETTING UP WORKPIECES	○	○	◉	○	○		◉	○	○	
MISSING PARTS	◉	○	○		○	○	◉		○	
WRONG PARTS	◉	◉	◉	◉	◉	◉	◉		◉	
PROCESSING WRONG WORKPIECE	○	◉	◉	○	○	◉	◉		○	
MISOPERATION			○				○		○	◉
ADJUSTMENT ERROR	○	○	○	◉	○	◉	○	○	○	○
IMPROPER EQUIPMENT SETUP			○				◉			◉
IMPROPER TOOLS AND JIGS			○				◉			○

All About Poka-yoke

What Are the Five Best Poka-yoke?

Human errors are usually inadvertent. Poka-yoke devices help us avoid defects, even when inadvertent errors are made. Poka-yoke help build quality into processes.

Here are five examples of poka-yoke for detecting or avoiding defects caused by human errors.

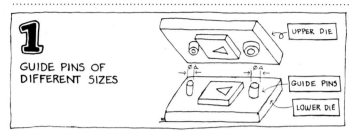

1 GUIDE PINS OF DIFFERENT SIZES

UPPER DIE

GUIDE PINS

LOWER DIE

2 ERROR DETECTION AND ALARMS

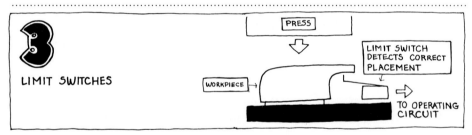

3 LIMIT SWITCHES

PRESS

LIMIT SWITCH DETECTS CORRECT PLACEMENT

WORKPIECE

TO OPERATING CIRCUIT

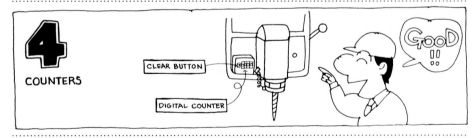

4 COUNTERS

CLEAR BUTTON

DIGITAL COUNTER

GOOD !!

5 CHECKLISTS

CHECKLIST

✔ MANUAL?

✔ KEYS?

✔ SPARE TIRE?

The Basic Functions of Poka-yoke

A defect exists in one of two states: It is either about to occur, or it has already occurred. Poka-yoke have three basic functions to use against defects — shutdown, control, and warning. Recognizing that a defect is about to occur is called "prediction," and recognizing that a defect has already occurred is called "detection." The following diagram shows the relationship of the two possible states of defects with the three functions of poka-yoke.

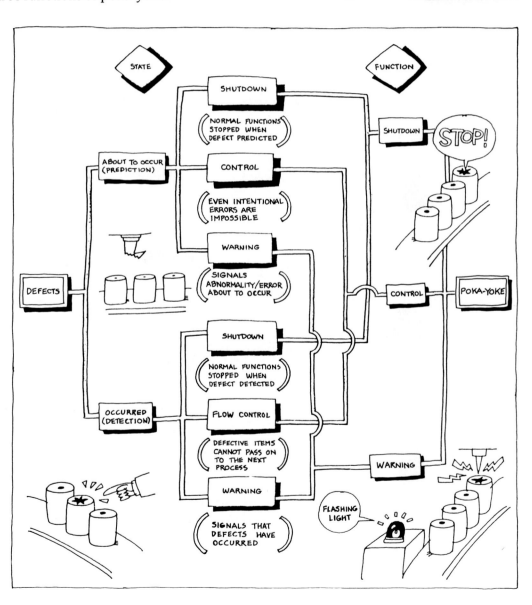

Poka-yoke Hints

1 IDENTIFY ITEMS BY THEIR CHARACTERISTICS

● **BY WEIGHT:**

ESTABLISH WEIGHT STANDARDS. USE A BALANCE OR SCALE TO IDENTIFY DEFECTIVE ITEMS.

● **BY DIMENSION:**

ESTABLISH STANDARDS FOR LENGTH, WIDTH, DIAMETER, ETC. IDENTIFY DIVERGENCE FROM STANDARDS BY USING STOPPERS IN JIGS, LIMIT SWITCHES, ETC.

● **BY SHAPE:**

ESTABLISH STANDARDS FOR SHAPE CHARACTERISTICS SUCH AS ANGLES, DEPRESSIONS, PROJECTIONS, CURVATURE, OR POSITION OF HOLES. IDENTIFY DIVERGENCE FROM STANDARDS WITH LIMIT SWITCH, CORRESPONDING LOCATOR PINS IN JIGS, INTERFERENCE PARTS IN DELIVERY CHUTES, ETC.

WHAT?

2 DETECT DEVIATION FROM PROCEDURES OR OMITTED PROCESSES

● PROCESS SEQUENCE METHOD:

THE SUBSEQUENT WORK CANNOT BE PERFORMED IF THE WORKER'S HAND OR MACHINE OPERATIONS DURING A PROCESS DO NOT FOLLOW THE STANDARD WORK PROCEDURES.

INCORRECT PROCEDURE

CUTTING   BENDING   CANNOT BE DRILLED AFTER BENDING

● PROCESS-TO-PROCESS SEQUENCE METHOD:

OPERATIONS CANNOT BE PERFORMED IF ONE OF A SERIES OF PROCESSES HAS BEEN OMITTED AND THE REGULAR PROCEDURES HAVE NOT BEEN FOLLOWED.

WE LEFT SOME PARTS OUT!

3 DETECT DEVIATIONS FROM FIXED VALUES

● USING A COUNTER:

A FIXED NUMBER, SUCH AS THE NUMBER OF OPERATIONS OR PARTS, IS USED AS A REFERENCE. IF THE ACTUAL NUMBER DIFFERS FROM THE REFERENCE NUMBER, AN ALARM SOUNDS.

PASSED 0007   FAILED

● ODD-PART-OUT METHOD:

WHEN A NUMBER OF PARTS ARE ASSEMBLED AS A LOT, THE EXACT NUMBER OF PARTS NEEDED IS PREPARED. WHEN THE LOT IS COMPLETED, LEFT-OVER PARTS SIGNAL THE OCCURANCE OF ERRORS.

LEFT-OVER PARTS

● CRITICAL CONDITION DETECTION:

A CRITICAL MANUFACTURING CONDITION SUCH AS PRESSURE, CURRENT, TEMPERATURE, OR TIME, IS MEASURED. WORK CANNOT PROCEED IF THE VALUE IS NOT WITHIN A PREDETERMINED RANGE.

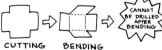

Detection Devices to Use for Poka-yoke

A wide variety of devices can be used to detect errors and defects. The detectors used for poka-yoke can be divided into those which contact the part being tested, and those which do not contact the part.

• Contact devices

Microswitches and *limit switches* are the most frequently used detection devices in poka-yoke. They can detect the presence of items such as workpieces, dies, or cutting tools and are very flexible. Limit switches can be used to ensure that a process does not begin until the workpiece is in the correct position, for example, or they can be used to stop a process if the workpiece has the wrong shape.

There are many other contact detection devices used in poka-yoke including proximity switches, positioning sensors, displacement sensors, metal-passage sensors, and a variety of mechanical devices.

SHAPE	TYPE	MOTION BEFORE OPERATION	MOTION AFTER OPERATION	FORCE REQUIRED	VIBRATIONS/ IMPACTS	CHARACTERISTICS
	PIN PUSH-BUTTON	SMALL	SMALL	LARGE	EXCELLENT	SUITABLE FOR LINEAR AND SHORT-STROKE OPERATIONS. DETECTS POSITIONS WITH THE HIGHEST PRECISION BECAUSE SNAP-ACTION MECHANISM IS ACTUATED DIRECTLY BY PIN PUSH-BUTTON. HOWEVER, IT HAS THE LEAST MOTION AFTER OPERATION, AND REQUIRES A RELIABLE STOPPER.
	PANEL-MOUNTED ROLLER PUSH-BUTTON	SMALL	LARGE	LARGE	ACCEPTABLE	SUITABLE FOR FAST-MOVING CAMS OR DOGS.
	HINGED LEVER	LARGE	MEDIUM	SMALL	ACCEPTABLE	OPERATES WITH A SMALL FORCE. SUITABLE FOR USE WITH LOW-SPEED CAMS OR DOGS. HAS A LARGE STROKE. LEVERS OF VARIOUS SHAPES CAN BE USED TO MATCH THE SHAPES OF THE PARTS BEING DETECTED.
	HINGED LEVER-ROLLER	LARGE	MEDIUM	SMALL	ACCEPTABLE	CAN BE USED WITH HIGH-SPEED CAMS OR DOGS. FORCE NEEDED TO OPERATE THE PIN PUSH-BUTTON DEPENDS ON LEVER RATIO. HAS A LARGE STROKE.
	HINGED LEVER-ROLLER OPERATING IN ONE DIRECTION	MEDIUM	MEDIUM	MEDIUM	ACCEPTABLE	CAN BE OPERATED BY A BODY MOVING IN ONLY ONE DIRECTION. IF FORCE IS APPLIED IN THE OPPOSITE DIRECTION, THE ROLLER PART FOLDS AND BECOMES INOPERATIVE.
	ROLLER-LEAF SPRING	MEDIUM	MEDIUM	MEDIUM	GOOD	ALSO CAN BE USED WITH HIGH-SPEED CAMS.

• Noncontact devices

Photoelectric switches can handle opaque, translucent, and transparent objects, depending upon the need. There are two types of detection possible. In the *transmission* type, two units are used, one to transmit a light beam, the other to receive the light beam. This type can be normally on, meaning light is unobstructed, or normally off, meaning light is not transmitted. The *reflecting* type of PE sensor responds to light reflected from an object to detect its presence.

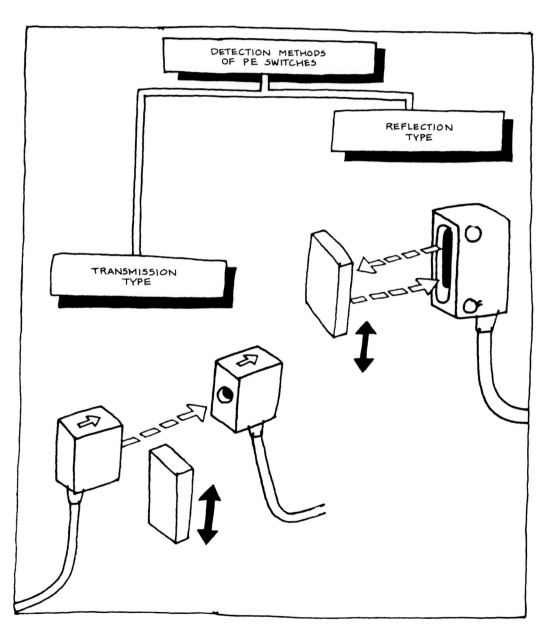

Typical Examples of Poka-yoke

• Processing omissions

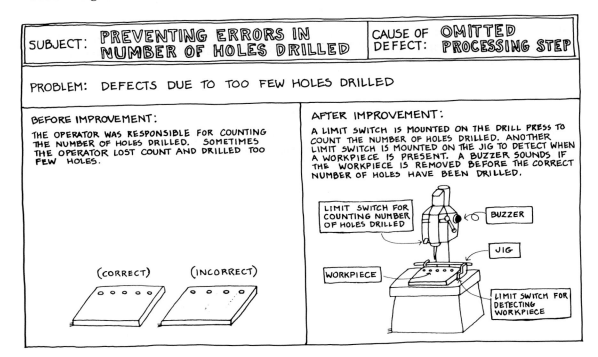

| SUBJECT: | PREVENTING ERRORS IN NUMBER OF HOLES DRILLED | CAUSE OF DEFECT: | OMITTED PROCESSING STEP |

PROBLEM: DEFECTS DUE TO TOO FEW HOLES DRILLED

BEFORE IMPROVEMENT:

THE OPERATOR WAS RESPONSIBLE FOR COUNTING THE NUMBER OF HOLES DRILLED. SOMETIMES THE OPERATOR LOST COUNT AND DRILLED TOO FEW HOLES.

(CORRECT)　(INCORRECT)

AFTER IMPROVEMENT:

A LIMIT SWITCH IS MOUNTED ON THE DRILL PRESS TO COUNT THE NUMBER OF HOLES DRILLED. ANOTHER LIMIT SWITCH IS MOUNTED ON THE JIG TO DETECT WHEN A WORKPIECE IS PRESENT. A BUZZER SOUNDS IF THE WORKPIECE IS REMOVED BEFORE THE CORRECT NUMBER OF HOLES HAVE BEEN DRILLED.

LIMIT SWITCH FOR COUNTING NUMBER OF HOLES DRILLED

BUZZER

JIG

WORKPIECE

LIMIT SWITCH FOR DETECTING WORKPIECE

• **Processing errors**

SUBJECT:	PREVENTING HOLE-DRILLING DEFECTS	CAUSE OF DEFECT:	PROCESSING ERRORS

PROBLEM: IN DRILLING PROCESSES USING A DRILL PRESS, THE DRILL WAS OFTEN WITHDRAWN BEFORE IT HAD GONE ALL THE WAY IN. THE RESULTING DRILLING DEFECTS CAUSED TROUBLE DURING ASSEMBLY.

BEFORE IMPROVEMENT:

THE PROCEDURE WAS TO LOWER THE DRILL UNTIL IT WENT ALL THE WAY THROUGH THE PART. SOMETIMES THE DRILL WAS RAISED BEFORE ACHIEVING THE REQUIRED DEPTH, RESULTING IN DEFECTIVE HOLES. IT WAS UP TO THE OPERATOR'S SKILL AND INTUITION TO TELL WHETHER THE HOLE WAS DRILLED PROPERLY. DEFECTIVE HOLES WERE NOT DISCOVERED UNTIL THE ASSEMBLY STAGE.

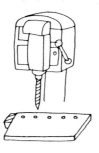

AFTER IMPROVEMENT:

TWO LIMIT SWITCHES WERE MOUNTED. DRILLING IS ASSUMED TO BE DEFECTIVE IF SWITCH 1 IS RELEASED BEFORE SWITCH 2 IS TRIPPED. IN THIS CASE A BUZZER SOUNDS TO NOTIFY THE OPERATOR.

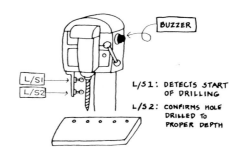

L/S1: DETECTS START OF DRILLING

L/S2: CONFIRMS HOLE DRILLED TO PROPER DEPTH

• Missing parts

SUBJECT:
PREVENTING OMISSION OF BUSHINGS

NATURE OF DEFECT: MISSING PARTS

PROBLEM:

BUSHINGS WERE TO BE INSERTED DURING DIE CASTING, BUT THEY WERE OFTEN OMITTED. FOR THIS REASON A SPECIAL INSPECTION PROCESS WAS PROVIDED, AND ALL OF THE ITEMS WERE INSPECTED VISUALLY. IN SPITE OF THIS, CUSTOMERS CONTINUED TO COMPLAIN OF MISSING BUSHINGS.

AFTER IMPROVEMENT:

A SENSOR WAS MOUNTED IN THE DEBURRING PROCESS FOLLOWING DIE CASTING AND INTERLOCKED WITH THE PRESS POWER CIRCUIT. THE PRESS WILL NOT OPERATE IF THE BUSHING HAS BEEN OMITTED. AT THE SAME TIME, AN ALARM SOUNDS AND A LAMP LIGHTS TO INFORM THE OPERATOR THAT THE BUSHING HAS BEEN OMITTED.

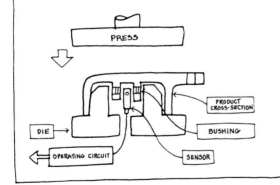

• Errors in setting up workpieces

SUBJECT:
PREVENTING HOLE-DRILLING DEFECTS

CAUSE OF DEFECT: ERROR IN SETTING WORKPIECE IN PLACE

PROBLEM:

IN DRILLING PROCESSES USING A DRILL PRESS, THE WORK-PIECE WAS OFTEN SET IN PLACE BACKWARDS, WHICH PRODUCED INCORRECT HOLE POSITIONS. THE DEFECTS WERE NOT DISCOVERED UNTIL ASSEMBLY.

AFTER IMPROVEMENT:

A LIMIT SWITCH WAS MOUNTED ON THE JIG TO DETECT GROOVES CUT ON TWO SIDES OF THE WORKPIECE. WHEN THE WORKPIECE IS BACKWARDS, THE LIMIT SWITCH IS ACTIVATED AND THE MACHINE CANNOT OPERATE. DEFECTS DUE TO DRILLING MISTAKES IN THIS PROCESS WERE COMPLETELY ELIMINATED, ACHIEVING ZERO DEFECTS.

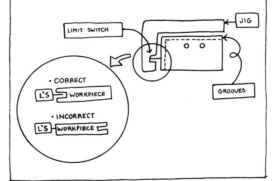

• Improper, damaged, or poorly designed jigs

SUBJECT: PREVENTING MOUNTING ERRORS WHEN MOUNTING DRAWER RAILS ON LEFT AND RIGHT CABINET SIDES

CAUSE OF DEFECT: INADEQUATE JIGS

PROBLEM:

IN THE PROCESS OF MOUNTING DRAWER RAILS ON CABINET SIDES, ERRORS OCCURRED WHEN THE MOUNTING JIGS SLIPPED, OR WHEN THE OPERATOR FORGOT TO REVERSE THE MOUNTING JIGS WHEN CHANGING FROM THE RIGHT TO THE LEFT SIDES.

AFTER IMPROVEMENT:

THE DRAWER RAIL MOUNTING JIGS WERE FASTENED IN PLACE SO THEY CANNOT SLIP. AT THE SAME TIME, THE JIG WAS MODIFIED SO IT IS IMPOSSIBLE TO MOUNT THE DRAWER RAILS WITHOUT REVERSING THE JIG FOR THE LEFT AND RIGHT SIDES.

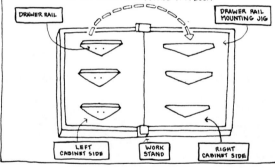

JIG IS FLIPPED LIKE A PAGE OF A BOOK

DRAWER RAIL

DRAWER RAIL MOUNTING JIG

LEFT CABINET SIDE

WORK STAND

RIGHT CABINET SIDE

• Using the wrong parts

SUBJECT: PREVENTING MOUNTING OF WRONG PARTS DURING ASSEMBLY

NATURE OF DEFECT: WRONG PARTS ASSEMBLED

PROBLEM:

IN THE ASSEMBLY PROCESS, MODELS WERE CHANGED SEVERAL TIMES A DAY, AND THE OPERATORS SOMETIMES MOUNTED THE WRONG ITEMS.

AFTER IMPROVEMENT:

A ROTATING PARTS RACK WAS MADE. IT HAS ONLY ONE DELIVERY OUTLET. WHEN THE MODEL BUTTON IS PRESSED, ONLY THOSE PARTS NEEDED FOR A PARTICULAR MODEL ARE AVAILABLE FROM THE DELIVERY OUTLET. THIS MAKES IT IMPOSSIBLE TO INSTALL PARTS FOR THE WRONG MODEL, EVEN ACCIDENTALLY.

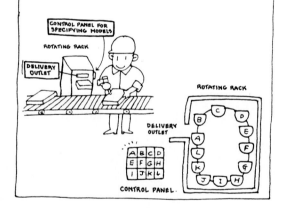

CONTROL PANEL FOR SPECIFYING MODELS

ROTATING RACK

DELIVERY OUTLET

ROTATING RACK

DELIVERY OUTLET

CONTROL PANEL

Achieving Mistake-proof, Zero-defect Manufacturing through Poka-yoke

The Eight Principles of Basic Improvement for Poka-yoke and Zero Defects

1. Build quality into processes

Make it impossible to turn out defective items even if an error is committed. The approach in this case is 100 percent inspection, using poka-yoke safeguards built into jigs and processes.

2. All inadvertent errors and defects can be eliminated

We must assume that mistakes are not inevitable. Where there is a powerful will, a way can be found to eliminate all errors and defects.

3. Stop doing it wrong and start doing it right — now!

Let's eliminate entirely the "buts" in statements like "we know that it is not right, but…"

4. Don't think up excuses, think about how to do it right

Rather than thinking up excuses, let's think about how things can be done right.

5. A 60% chance of success is good enough — implement your idea now!

In improvements, there is no need to aim for perfection before taking action. Analyze the cause and think of a solution. If your solution has better than a 50-50 chance of succeeding, implement it right away. You can change or further refine your solution based on the facts that result from implementing it right off.

6. Mistakes and defects can be reduced to zero when everyone works together to eliminate them

Zero mistakes and zero defects cannot be achieved by one person alone. It is important for everyone in the entire company to work together to eliminate mistakes and defects.

7. Ten heads are better than one

The brainstorm of any one individual is important, but the wisdom and creativity that comes through the efforts of ten people is more valuable. Teamwork is the key to effective improvement ideas.

8. Seek out the true cause, using 5 W's and one H

Should a defect occur, *do not* demand more inspectors. Instead, get to the root of the problem to ensure that the countermeasure applied is a real solution, and not just a bandage. Ask "Why did the defect occur?" and to the answer you get, ask "Why?" again. Don't be satisfied with causes that come to mind easily. Ask "Why?" at least five times to discover the roots of the problem. Only then ask "How do we fix it?" and put the solution into practice.

A Company-wide Mistake-proofing, Zero Defect Effort

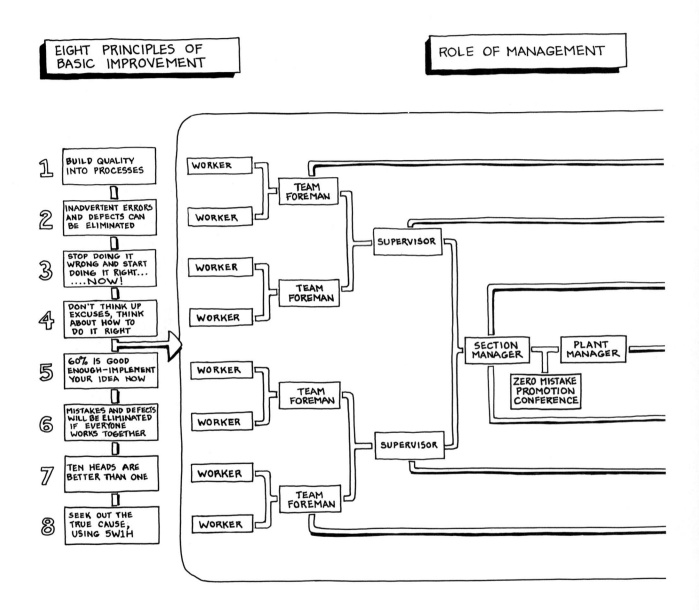

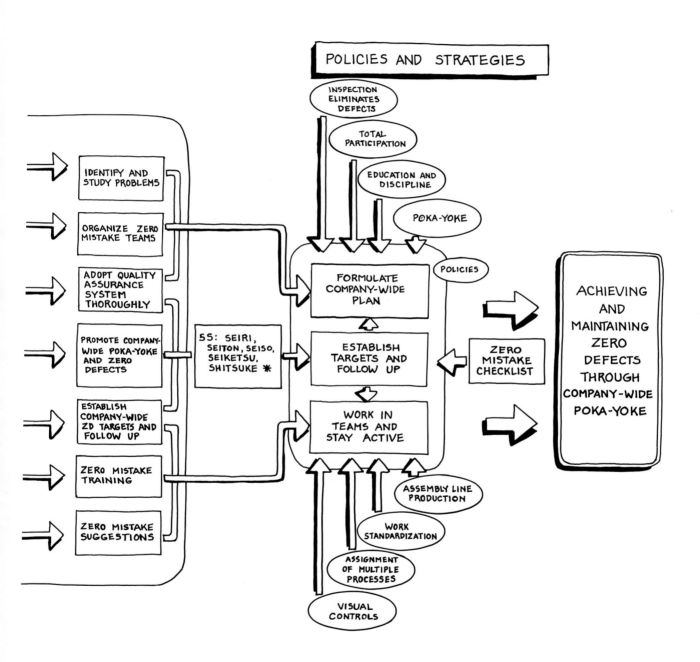

* The "five S's" are key concepts of industrial housekeeping that begin with "S" in Japanese. They are: *seiri* (organization), *seiton* (orderliness), *seiso* (the act of cleaning), *seiketsu* (the state of cleanliness), and *shitsuke* (the practice of discipline).

Zero Defect Strategies for Factories

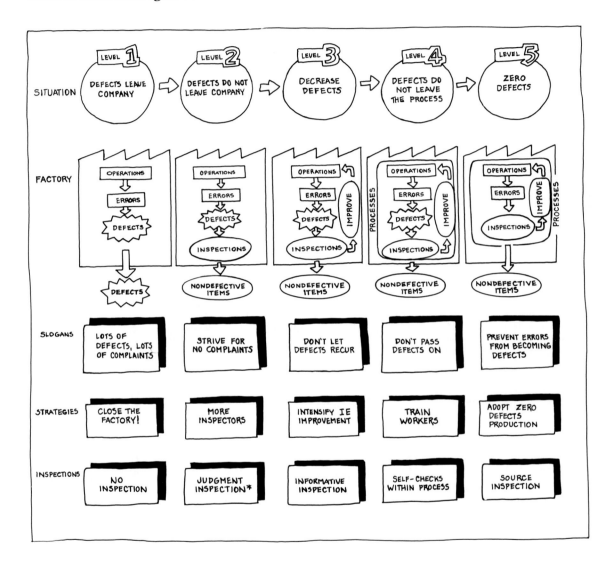

* Judgment inspection is comparison with a standard; this identifies defects, but does not reduce them. By giving feedback to the work process, an informative inspection can lower the defect rate. An advanced form of informative inspection is the self-check system. Often using poka-yoke devices, a self-check cuts the feedback time by discovering defects before the product leaves the process. Source inspection skips the feedback stage and catches errors at their source to prevent them from becoming defects in the first place. For more on these concepts, see Shigeo Shingo, *Zero Quality Control: Source Inspection and the Poka-yoke System*, Cambridge, MA: Productivity Press, 1986.

240 Poka-yoke Examples

Poka-yoke eliminates waste in operations and complaints from consumers, and creates a profitable factory. The 240 examples of poka-yoke that follow were collected from more than 100 companies in 10 different industries, including electronics, automobiles, cameras, and heavy industry.

Processing Errors

● *Example 1*

Process: Series of operations performed by one worker

Problem: Omitted processing

Solution: Interlock operations

Prevent Error:

Detect Error: X

Shutdown: X

Control:

Alarm: X

Key Improvement: Process will not start if preceding operation is omitted

Description of Process: One operator performs several different operations, including drilling, tapping, press-fitting, and rinsing, in round-robin fashion on nine machines.

Before Improvement:

Because of the complexity of the line, newly assigned workers often did not fully understand the requirements of the work. Some unprocessed items were passed to the next operation because the operator had forgotten to press a start-up switch along the line. The unprocessed items numbered two or three a day.

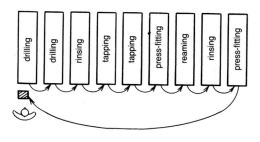

After Improvement:

The switches for the different operations were interlocked to make it impossible to start a new round of processing if any of the operations in the preceding round has been omitted. In addition, as each operation is started, a corresponding lamp is lit on a panel. After one cycle is finished, the worker returns to the first operation to begin a new cycle of processing. If no operations have been skipped, the switch for the first operation is not locked, and the operator can begin a new cycle. However, if an operation has been omitted, the switch for the first operation is locked. The operator observes the lamps to determine which operation has been skipped. (A skipped operation turns on a buzzer and a rotating warning light.)

The worker then goes to the operation for which the lamp is not lit, switches that machine onto a manual circuit, and performs that operation alone. When the operation is finished, the worker resets the machine to the automatic circuit and starts the first operation in the series.

lamps indicating completion of processing

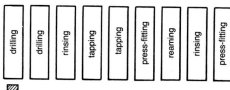

● *Example 2*

Process: Tapping

Problem: Holes not tapped, or not tapped to proper depth

Solution: Limit switches detect tapping depth errors

Prevent Error:

Detect Error: X

Shutdown: X

Control:

Alarm: X

Key Improvement: Tool modified to guarantee correct processing

Description of Process: Deep (38 mm) holes are tapped in high carbon steel.

Before Improvement:

The tap was driven to the desired depth in one operation. However, the hard material and extreme tapping depth caused the clutch of the machine to slip if the tap was slightly worn, and tapping stopped before the hole had been tapped to the required depth. The operator was unable to detect this defect.

After Improvement:

Limit switches were mounted at the front and back of the tapping machine's main shaft, enabling the operator to check the movement of the shaft. If the main shaft does not go down to the prescribed depth, a blinking red lamp comes on to alert the operator. The machine cannot be started again until the operator has dealt with the defective workpiece and cleared the error.

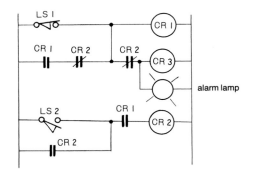

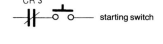

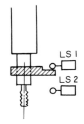

● *Example 3*

Process: Drilling

Problem: Workpiece set into jig incorrectly

Solution: Use air cylinder to position workpiece

Key Improvement: Jig modified to guarantee correct positioning

Prevent Error: X

Detect Error:

Shutdown:

Control: X

Alarm:

Description of Process: A workpiece is placed in a jig and drilled.

Before Improvement:

The drilling jig had a reference pin for positioning the workpiece, but the operator sometimes forgot to move the workpiece into contact with the pin. The operator went ahead with the drilling, assuming that the part was in the correct position. This resulted in holes drilled in the wrong position, making the item defective.

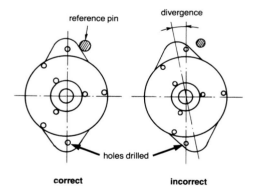

After Improvement:

An air cylinder was installed on the jig to press the workpiece against the reference pin after it is mounted.

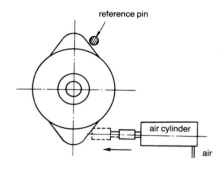

● *Example 4*

Process:	Countersinking	**Prevent Error:** X	**Shutdown:**	
Problem:	Countersinking was omitted	**Detect Error:**	**Control:**	X
Solution:	Modify hole punch to make and countersink hole in one operation		**Alarm:**	

Key Improvement: Tool modified to guarantee correct process

Description of Process: Countersinking is specified for holes punched in radiator plates.

Before Improvement:

After punching, the holes were countersunk with a drill press, but there were variations in the dimensions and the processing was sometimes omitted.

After Improvement:

The punch was remodeled to punch and countersink the hole in one operation. Dimensional variations and omissions are completely eliminated and the processing time is shortened, killing two birds with one stone. The only costs are for remodeling the punch.

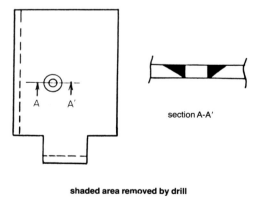

section A-A'

shaded area removed by drill

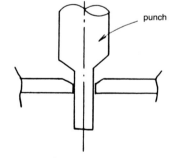

punch

punch shape improved

● *Example 5*

Process: Riveting

Problem: Right angle of plate deformed

Solution: Improve jig

Key Improvement: Jig modified to guarantee correct positioning

Prevent Error: X

Detect Error:

Shutdown:

Control: X

Alarm:

Description of Process: Pins are riveted to a plate near an inside right angle corner.

Before Improvement:	After Improvement:
The riveting operation often bent the corner into an oblique angle.	After reexamining how the defect occurred, a guide was installed on the jig to keep the plate at the proper angle during riveting.

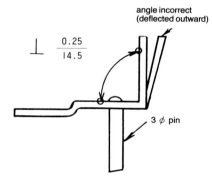

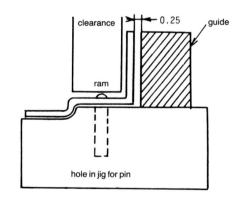

● *Example 6*

Process: Mounting cassette transport covers

Prevent Error: X

Shutdown:

Problem: Plastic covers were scratched when screw-driver slipped out of screw slots

Detect Error:

Control: X

Solution: Change shape of screw slots

Alarm:

Key Improvement: Part modified to protect it from damage

Description of Process: Plastic cassette transport covers are assembled with screws.

Before Improvement:

Cassette covers were frequently scratched when the screwdriver slipped out of the screw slot and slid against the plastic covers.

After Improvement:

The cause of the trouble was scrutinized and a change was made in the shape of the screw slot to prevent the screwdriver from slipping. Scratches caused by the screwdriver slipping have been completely eliminated.

● *Example 7*

Process: Press molding

Problem: Molded products left in press

Solution: Photoelectric detection of molded products in press

Key Improvement: Tool modified to protect it from damage

Prevent Error: X

Detect Error:

Shutdown: X

Control:

Alarm:

Description of Process: Products were molded on a press.

Before Improvement:

   Sleepy night-shift operators sometimes forgot to remove molded products before operating the press again. Because correct operation relied on the workers' vigilance, die failures or defective products occurred about once a month.

After Improvement:

   A photoelectric switch is used to detect the presence of molded products. If molded products remain in the press, the switch is disabled and the press cannot be operated. Smashing of molded products and die failures are completely eliminated.

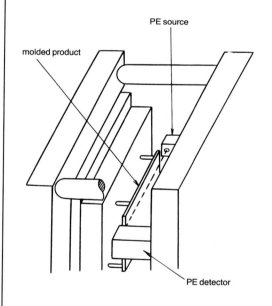

molded product

PE source

PE detector

● Example 8

Process: Staking a shaft to a plate

Problem: Shaft reversed end to end

Solution: Make ends of shaft interchangeable

Key Improvement: Part modified to guarantee correct positioning

Prevent Error: X

Detect Error:

Shutdown:

Control: X

Alarm:

Description of Process: A shaft is joined to a chassis by staking.

Before Improvement:

One end of the shaft was grooved for an E-ring, while the other end had no groove. Aside from that difference the shaft was symmetrical and the operator could join the shaft to the chassis with either end free. This resulted in errors that made it impossible to mount the E-ring during later assembly.

After Improvement:

Both ends of the shaft are now grooved for an E-ring, so either end can be staked to the chassis without creating an error. The E-ring can always be mounted and it is impossible to create a defect.

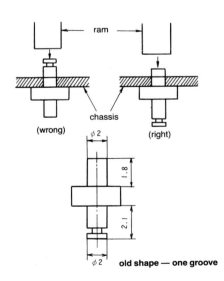

old shape — one groove

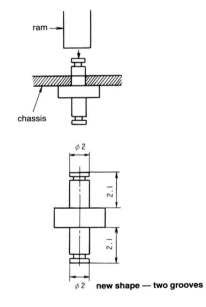

new shape — two grooves

● *Example 9*

Process: Joining a shaft to a control arm

Problem: Wrong end of shaft inserted

Solution: Change size of hole and shaft to prevent errors

Key Improvement: Part modified to guarantee correct positioning

Prevent Error: X

Detect Error:

Shutdown:

Control: X

Alarm:

Description of Process: A shaft is pressed into a press hole in a control arm.

Before Improvement:

The two ends of the shaft had the same diameter, and either end could be pressed into the hole. Shafts were often pressed into the hole backwards.

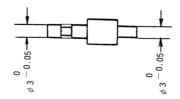

After Improvement:

The diameters of the press hole and the end of the shaft to be pressed were made smaller so that the other end does not fit the press hole. The danger of backward press-fitting is completely eliminated.

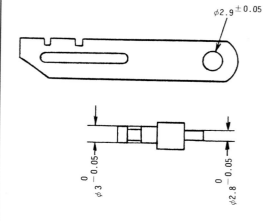

● *Example 10*

Process: Staking

Problem: Component joined to wrong side of plate or omitted altogether

Solution: Install limit switch on subsequent process to detect proper staking

Key Improvement: Tool modified to detect defective parts

Prevent Error:

Detect Error: X

Shutdown:

Control: X

Alarm:

Description of Process: A shaft-like component is staked into a hole in a plate.

Before Improvement:

It was possible to stake the component to the wrong side of the plate or to omit it altogether.

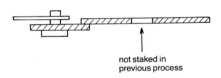

not staked in previous process

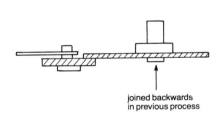

joined backwards in previous process

After Improvement:

The subsequent process was equipped with a microswitch so the machine will not operate if the component is not staked or is joined to the wrong side in the previous process. Pieces with these defects are no longer passed on down the line.

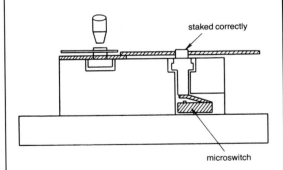

staked correctly

microswitch

● *Example 11*

Process: Processing chassis

Problem: Chassis set backwards in jig

Solution: Additional guide pin taking advantage of asymmetry

Key Improvement: Jig modified to guarantee correct positioning

Prevent Error: X

Detect Error:

Shutdown:

Control: X

Alarm:

Description of Process: A chassis was placed in a jig for machining.

Before Improvement:

It was possible to insert the chassis in the jig backwards. Correct operation depended on the worker's vigilance.

After Improvement:

A guide pin was added, keyed to an asymmetrical feature of the chassis. This completely eliminates the danger of backward processing.

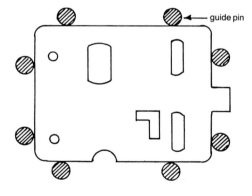

guide pin

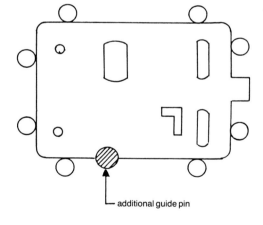

additional guide pin

● *Example 12*

Process: Riveting coupling bars

Problem: One bar joined upside down

Solution: Add guide pin to riveting jig

Key Improvement: Jig modified to guarantee correct positioning

Prevent Error: X

Detect Error:

Shutdown:

Control: X

Alarm:

Description of Process: Two bars are riveted together.

Before Improvement:

    The bottom bar has a round hole on one end and an elliptical one on the other. It was possible to put the bar on the jig with the holes on the wrong sides and to join them that way, resulting in defects.

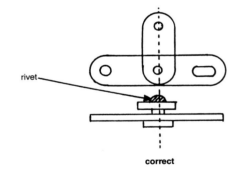

rivet

correct

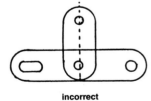

incorrect

After Improvement:

    An elliptical preventive pin was added to the jig so that the bar cannot be seated on the jig in the wrong direction. Backward riveting is completely eliminated.

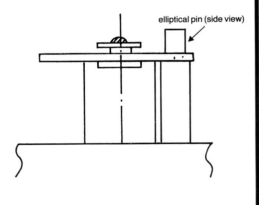

elliptical pin (side view)

● *Example 13*

Process: Punching holes in shield cases

Problem: Holes punched in wrong positions

Solution: Make shield cases asymmetrical and add extra guide pin

Key Improvement: Part and jig modified to guarantee correct positioning

Prevent Error: X

Detect Error:

Shutdown:

Control: X

Alarm:

Description of Process: Shield cases are set on a jig and square holes are punched out.

Before Improvement:

Since the cases were symmetrical, they could be set into the jig in reverse, and the square holes were often punched in the wrong positions.

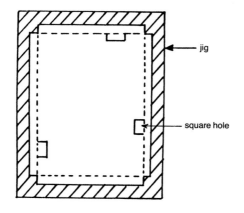

After Improvement:

A round hole was designed into the case in an asymmetrical position, and a corresponding guide pin is mounted on the jig. The risk of punching square holes in the wrong places is completely eliminated.

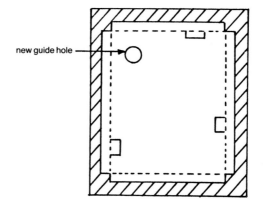

● Example 14

Process:	A series of processes involving silver-lined phosphor bronze sheet	**Prevent Error:** X	**Shutdown:**
Problem:	Multiple positional errors	**Detect Error:**	**Control:** X
Solution:	Visual indicators of correct setup		**Alarm:**

Key Improvement: Examples of correct processing provided as guides

Description of Process: Sheet stock of silver-lined phosphor bronze undergoes a series of operations to form the final product. The stock is first punched on a press, then press-bent (the usual practice is to perform these operations at the same time using sequential-feed or tandem-feed dies). The parts are then annealed and riveted to other parts.

Before Improvement:

In each process errors occurred when the part was processed upside down or set incorrectly in the jig. The parts were pressed from the sheet upside down, or bent upside down, or the pins were riveted in the wrong hole or to the wrong side.

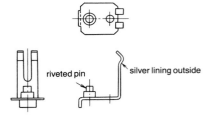

riveted pin

silver lining outside

After Improvement:

Several different safeguards were installed to help the workers make visual checks that processing is proceeding correctly.

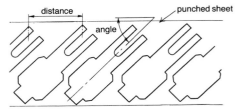

distance — angle — punched sheet

1. A sheet that has been punched out is attached to the front surface of the press as an example. By referring to this, the operator can tell both the processing distance and the correct angle. This prevents errors when positioning the sheet for punching the outer shape.

2. A correctly bent sample is also attached to the press. The operator can easily see the correct direction to bend the part. This prevents errors in bending direction.

punched sheet example

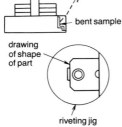

bent sample

drawing of shape of part

3. A picture of the shape of the parts is drawn on the riveting jig so the operator can see which of the two holes the pin fits in and which side is the front. This prevents errors in riveting and connecting the part to other parts.

riveting jig

● *Example 15*

Process: Drilling a variety of different workpieces

Problem: Errors made during setup for different workpieces

Solution: Eliminate setups

Prevent Error: X

Detect Error:

Shutdown:

Control: X

Alarm:

Key Improvement: Jig modified to guarantee correct positioning

Description of Process: Four mounting holes are drilled in many different types of plates. The holes are all equally spaced in one dimension, but are spaced differently along the other axis, depending on the size of the plate.

Before Improvement:

The holes were drilled with a four-spindle drill press, which required setup for each different type of plate. When the number of types of plates increased, time required for setup increased as well, and setup errors increased, resulting in incorrectly drilled holes.

After Improvement:

A new method for drilling the mounting plates was developed that makes setup operations unnecessary and completely eliminates defects in hole spacing. A two-spindle drill press is set to the constant hole spacing used in all the plates. A stop block is located on the drill press table in line with the spindles, and the jigs for the different plates now have notches at each hole position. The block fits into the notch in the jig as each plate is fed in. It is now possible to continuously feed the workpieces and position them accurately.

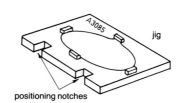
positioning notches

jig

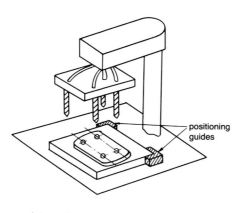
positioning guides

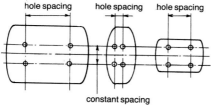
hole spacing   hole spacing   hole spacing

constant spacing

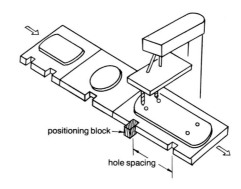
positioning block

hole spacing

● *Example 16*

Process: Laminating

Problem: Glue adhering to roller

Solution: Moisten roller to prevent glue from sticking

Key Improvement: Tool modified to protect it from damage

Prevent Error: X

Detect Error:

Shutdown:

Control: X

Alarm:

Description of Process: In a certain process, a metal roller is used to laminate two surfaces bonded with hot melted glue.

Before Improvement:

The glue tended to adhere to the steel roller. The adhering glue made impressions on the top surface of the laminate, resulting in defects. The machine was stopped every twenty to thirty minutes to remove the glue, but defective products continued to amount to as much as 50 percent of the total output.

After Improvement:

After an investigation into what conditions would prevent the glue from sticking to the steel roller, it was discovered that if the steel roller is dampened, the glue will not stick. A secondary roller is now used to dampen the steel roller during the lamination process, preventing the glue from adhering to the steel roller. As a result, defects caused by impressions are completely eliminated and productivity is improved almost fourfold.

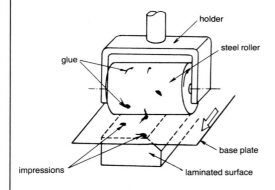

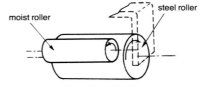

● *Example 17*

Process: Mounting nuts

Problem: Nuts missing or improperly positioned

Solution: Limit switch detector

Key Improvement: Tool modified to detect defective parts

Prevent Error:

Detect Error: X

Shutdown: X

Control:

Alarm:

Description of Process: A dedicated machine is used for mounting nuts onto parts for numerous different models.

Before Improvement:

Omission of nuts or faulty centering of nuts occurred and caused trouble during later assembly. A clamp was used to check for missing nuts, but faulty nut centering could not be detected.

After Improvement:

The machine power was connected to a limit switch that is actuated by a spring-mounted rod. If the nut is missing, the rod goes through the hole and the limit switch remains off. On the other hand, if the nut is off-center, the rod cannot rise at all, and the limit switch also stays off. If the nut is positioned correctly, the rod rises enough to turn on the limit switch, but no further. Selection switches are used to change the settings for different models.

rotates
top
bottom

clamp and bracket to check for missing nuts

M6 nut

limit switch

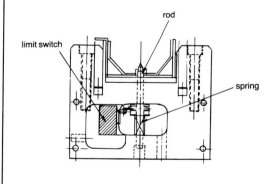

rod

limit switch

spring

● *Example 18*

Process: Roll-forming threads

Problem: Operation omitted or defective

Solution: Limit switch to detect omitted operation; use of more appropriate section of part for reference

Key Improvement: Jig modified to guarantee correct positioning; tool modified to detect defective parts

Prevent Error: X

Detect Error: X

Shutdown: X

Control: X

Alarm:

Description of Process: A two-spindle roll-forming machine is used to cut threads in a certain part.

Before Improvement:

Products with defective threads were produced because the guide had enough clearance that the workpiece could shift during forming. In addition, when the machine was started up after an emergency shutdown or a power loss, unthreaded parts were ejected at first. Items with faulty threads and items with no threads cut were sorted out by the workers, but some defects got by.

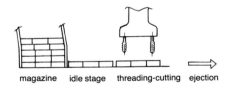

magazine   idle stage   threading-cutting   ejection

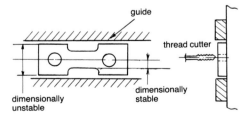

guide

thread cutter

dimensionally stable

dimensionally unstable

After Improvement:

Correctly threaded items, unthreaded items, and items with faulty taps all have different hole diameters. A device that checks the inner diameter of the holes and a limit switch circuit to shut off the threading operation are used together to eliminate defects and prevent the occurrence of defective items at the beginning of work.

1. Hole diameter before threading ϕ 7.3
   Hole diameter if threading is faulty ϕ 7.5
   Hole diameter if threading is good ϕ 6.8
   Check pin diameter ϕ 7.0

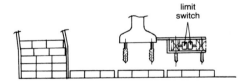

limit switch

2. A limit switch circuit is added to detect omitted or faulty threading.

3. The guide is revised, adding blocks to hold the workpiece in a stable position for threading.

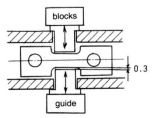

blocks

0.3

guide

● *Example 19*

Process: Tapping with multispindle tapping machine   **Prevent Error:**   **Shutdown:** X

Problem: Defective or omitted tapping   **Detect Error:** X   **Control:**

Solution: Limit switches detect correct tapping   **Alarm:**

Key Improvement: Tool modified to guarantee correct processing

Description of Process: Ten holes are tapped simultaneously on a multispindle tapping machine. If a tap breaks, or becomes worn, tapping will be defective or omitted.

Before Improvement:

The workers' vigilance was relied on to detect errors. Operators often failed to notice problems and workpieces sometimes passed onto the next process with defects. Every time this happened, the line shut down at a later process.

After Improvement:

Microswitches were installed under each tap drill, and the machine shuts down if any of the ten drills fails to actuate its switch.

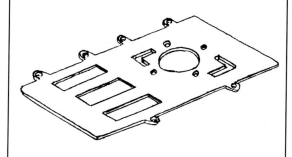

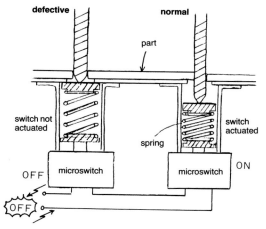

● *Example 20*

Process: Drilling

Problem: Missing holes

Solution: Hole detector before next process

Key Improvement: Tool modified to detect defective parts

Prevent Error:

Detect Error: X

Shutdown: X

Control:

Alarm:

Description of Process: Several holes are drilled in a plate in the preceding process. The holes are then finished using a multispindle drill press.

Before Improvement:

When an unprocessed item produced by the drilling machine in a preceding process came to the hole-finishing process, the finishing drills often broke. If this went unnoticed, all of the workpieces that came along the line afterward would have unfinished holes. It was extremely troublesome to process these defective workpieces afterward.

After Improvement:

A set of hole-detecting pins was mounted on the hole-finishing machine to detect the presence of holes in the next part while the current part is being processed. The pins are connected to limit switches that shut down the finishing machine if holes are not detected in the next part.

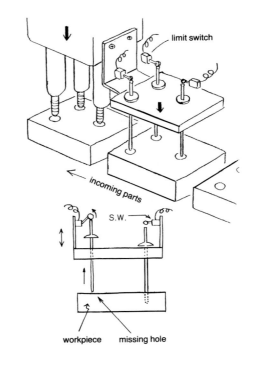

● *Example 21*

Process: Bending stamped parts

Problem: Parts bent upside down

Solution: Use cloth-lined chute to stop upside-down parts

Key Improvement: Chute modified to guarantee correct positioning

Prevent Error: X

Detect Error:

Shutdown:

Control: X

Alarm:

Description of Process: In this process, punched parts are bent to shape, with the burr resulting from punching on the inside of the bend.

Before Improvement:

The worker checked the orientation of the parts before bending each time but inevitably made errors.

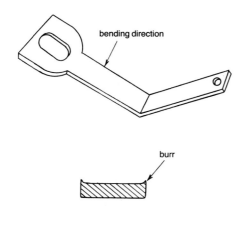

bending direction

burr

After Improvement:

After punching, the parts are slid down a chute lined with cloth. If the burrs are on the bottom of the piece (improper position for bending), they catch on the cloth and do not slide to the bottom of the chute. The parts that reach the bottom have the burr side up and can be pressed immediately.

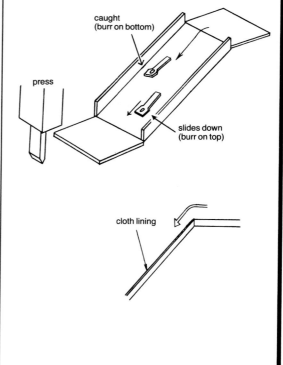

caught
(burr on bottom)

press

slides down
(burr on top)

cloth lining

● *Example 22*

Process: Processing wire stock

Problem: Deposits of foreign matter on stock and variations in wire dimensions

Solution: Stopper on wire feeder halts process if wire is out of dimension

Key Improvement: Tool modified to protect it from damage

Prevent Error: X

Detect Error:

Shutdown: X

Control:

Alarm:

Description of Process: Wire stock is sometimes produced with shape or dimensional variations or with foreign matter stuck to the stock. When this defective stock is processed, these variations must be detected to prevent defective products.

Before Improvement:

Deposits of foreign matter or variations of the wire stock dimensions made the motor stall when the wire stock entered the processing machine.

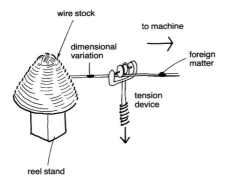

After Improvement:

If there is any foreign matter or a shape or dimensional variation on the wire, a stopper on the feed device catches on the wire at that place and moves along with the wire. The machine stops automatically when the stopper strikes a limit switch inside the machine.

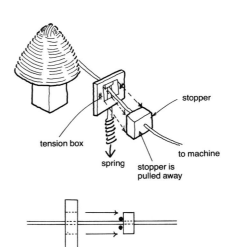

● *Example 23*

Process: Milling molded items

Problem: Unprocessed items

Solution: Use dimensional differences to detect unprocessed items in delivery chute

Key Improvement: Chute modified to detect defective parts

Prevent Error:

Detect Error: X

Alarm:

Shutdown:

Control: X

Description of Process: Molded items are milled in an automatic machine and delivered to the next process via a chute.

Before Improvement:

If an unmilled part came through the chute, the next machine shut down abnormally and could be damaged.

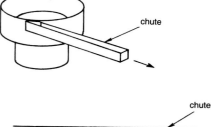

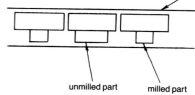

After Improvement:

A method was devised to use the geometrical shape of the unmilled parts to stop them if they come along. The feed chute is modified so that an unmilled part is caught by a block installed in the chute and is not delivered to the next machine. Damage to the machinery is prevented.

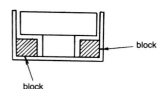

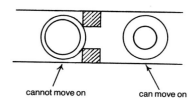

● *Example 24*

Process: Press-fitting capacitors

Problem: Capacitor improperly positioned

Solution: Jig with limit switch

Key Improvement: Jig used to guarantee correct positioning

Prevent Error: X

Detect Error:

Shutdown: X

Control:

Alarm:

Description of Process: Capacitors are press-fitted to a workpiece.

Before Improvement:

The worker determined the press-fitting position visually and the workpiece was often positioned inaccurately. Defects such as bending or damage occurred.

After Improvement:

A jig was made to position the workpiece and capacitor. The wiring is also changed so that the press cannot be activated until the limit switch is actuated by proper positioning. This eliminates the processing errors.

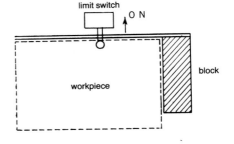

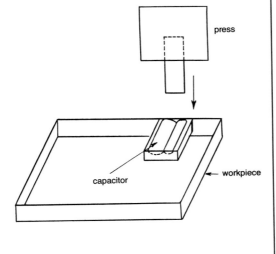

● *Example 25*

Process: Press-fitting bellows seals to O-rings

Problem: Faulty alignment

Solution: Jig to ensure correct alignment

Key Improvement: Jig to guarantee correct positioning

Prevent Error: X

Detect Error:

Shutdown: X

Control:

Alarm:

Description of Process: Bellows seals are press-fitted to O-rings.

Before Improvement:

The alignment between the bellows seals and the O-rings was determined visually. Variations of the press-fitting depth and deformations of the bellows seals often occurred as a result.

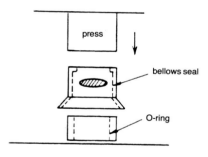

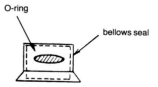

After Improvement:

A guide was installed so the bellows seals are always press-fitted uniformly. The press cannot be actuated unless a lever protruding from the guide has been inserted into the oblong notch in the bellows seal. This makes it possible to perform the press-fitting accurately.

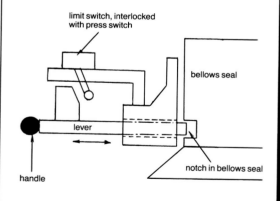

● *Example 26*

Process: Various

Problem: Worn pattern templates

Solution: Mark templates to make visual inspection easy

Key Improvement: Gage used for inspection

Prevent Error: X

Detect Error:

Shutdown:

Control: X

Alarm:

Description of Process: Sheet metal pattern templates for cutting garment pieces sometimes become damaged during use. It is important to maintain accurate templates so the garments will fit properly when assembled.

Before Improvement:

It was difficult to determine whether the template was worn and needed repairing, and inaccurate garment pieces were cut as a result.

After Improvement:

Using a guide, a stylus is used to scribe a line 1 mm in from the edge of the template when the template is new. After the template is used, the worker visually inspects this margin. Any variations, especially nicks and dents, are easy to detect. If there is any damage (if the interval is less than 1 mm), the template is repaired. This method is fast and easy because it uses visual inspection and is simple to understand.

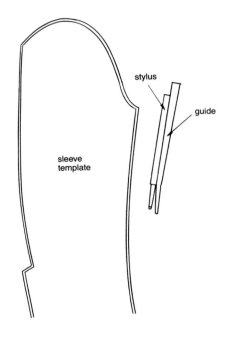

stylus

guide

sleeve
template

● *Example 27*

Process: Sewing buttons onto suit jacket cuffs

Problem: Buttons unevenly spaced

Solution: Jig

Key Improvement: Jig used to guarantee correct positioning

Prevent Error: X

Detect Error:

Shutdown:

Control: X

Alarm:

Description of Process: Some jacket cuffs have two buttons, others have three, and still others have four, depending on the design. The buttons are sewn on the cuffs one at a time using a large sewing machine.

Before Improvement:

The operator made marks at each button position and then sewed the buttons on, following the marks. However, partly because of problems with the sewing machine mechanism, and also due to the viewing angle, buttons were not sewn exactly at the right positions, resulting in uneven space between the buttons.

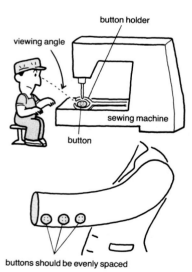

After Improvement:

A positioning jig was developed for sewing buttons. Now cuffs are positioned for buttons merely by putting the cuff end against the jig mounted on the sewing machine. This positions the cuff accurately for the required number of buttons and they come out neatly in a row.

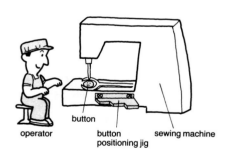

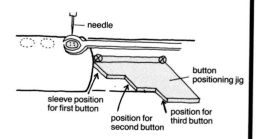

● *Example 28*

Process: Camera lens assembly

Problem: Crimping omitted

Solution: Photoelectric switch interlocked with crimping machine switch

Key Improvement: Tool modified to guarantee correct processing

Prevent Error: X

Detect Error:

Shutdown:

Control:

Alarm: X

Description of Process: The glass camera lens is assembled to the camera lens cone using a crimping machine.

Before Improvement:

After the operators set the lens in the lens cone and set the assembly in position on the crimping machine, they sometimes forgot to press the switch to start the process. As a result, the lens sometimes went on to the next process without being sealed into the lens cone.

After Improvement:

A reflecting-type photoelectric switch was mounted on the crimping machine, interlocked with the ON switch. The photoelectric switch is actuated when the metal lens cone is set in position in the jig of the crimping machine, and is released when the ON switch is pressed. If the operator forgets to press the switch, a buzzer sounds.

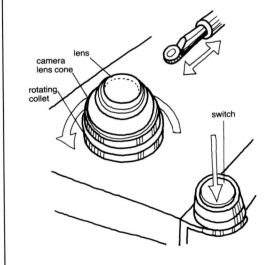

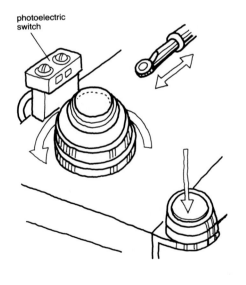

● *Example 29*

Process: Various

Problem: Following instructions for wrong process

Solution: Reorganize instruction charts

Key Improvement: Tool modified to guarantee correct processing

Prevent Error: X

Detect Error:

Shutdown:

Control: X

Alarm:

Description of Process: Ten operations are covered by a group of instruction charts. The operator performs processing while consulting the dimensions listed for each operation.

Before Improvement:

The operator was able to read instructions for the other operations while performing a given operation, since the instruction charts just sat on the workbench. Mistakes sometimes occurred because the operator accidentally followed the instructions for a different operation, such as using the dimensions for Step 2 while performing Step 1.

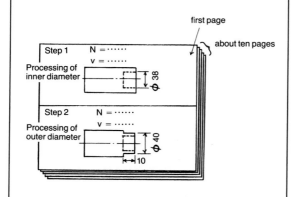

After Improvement:

The instruction charts were bound into a single file so the operator can see only the instructions for the operation being performed. The cover of the file is attached to a plate so the file can be propped open at an angle on the bench. To go on to the next process, the operator turns the page in the direction indicated by the arrow. Defects were completely eliminated.

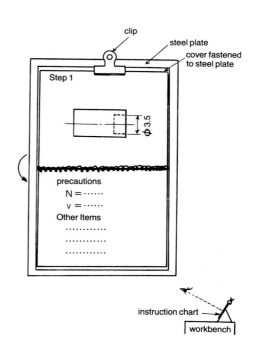

● *Example 30*

Process: Rinsing lenses

Problem: Scratched lenses

Solution: Change position of lenses in lens holder

Key Improvement: Procedure modified to protect part from damage

Prevent Error: X

Detect Error:

Shutdown:

Control: X

Alarm:

Description of Process: Lenses are inserted into a rinsing rack and passed through a rinsing machine.

Before Improvement:

The lenses were inserted vertically into the plastic rinsing rack. Inspection of some sharply curved lenses after rinsing sometimes showed that they had scratches around their circumferences. Scratching was caused by the plastic rack blades striking the lenses because of vibrations during rinsing.

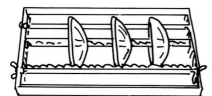

After Improvement:

It was discovered that the scratching does not occur when the lenses are inclined at an angle when inserted in the rinsing rack, which eliminates the movement of the lenses due to vibrations.

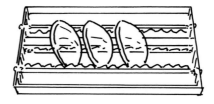

● *Example 31*

Process: Clinching pierce nuts

Problem: Nuts driven with insufficient pressure

Solution: Press marks workpiece if nuts are driven correctly

Key Improvement: Tool modified to guarantee correct processing

Prevent Error:

Detect Error: X

Shutdown:

Control: X

Alarm:

Description of Process: Pierce nuts are driven into workpieces using a press. The nuts are correctly driven when the press has descended to bottom dead center.

Before Improvement:

If mistakes were made when setting the press stroke, the pierce nuts would not be clinched onto the workpieces with sufficient force. Sometimes the nuts dropped out when the bolts were mounted and tightened during assembly.

After Improvement:

The die was redesigned so that it marks the workpiece when the nuts are driven in. The mark is made only if the nuts are driven to bottom dead center, so it is possible to determine at a glance whether the nuts have been sufficiently clinched. Nuts no longer drop out in subsequent processes.

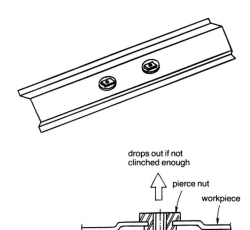

drops out if not
clinched enough

pierce nut

workpiece

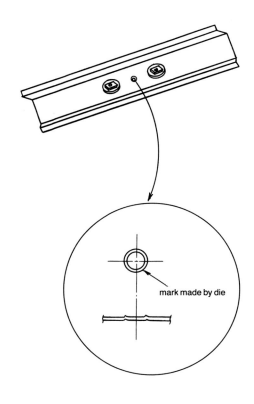

mark made by die

● Example 32

Process:	Checking for residual sand after casting intake manifolds	**Prevent Error:** X	**Shutdown:** X
Problem:	Balls used for testing were miscounted	**Detect Error:**	**Control:**
Solution:	Limit switch used to signal when all balls are present	**Alarm:** X	

Key Improvement: Operation tied to value of critical physical quantity

Description of Process: After casting and cleaning, intake manifolds for automobile engines are inspected for residual sand by passing eight small balls through the eight holes in the manifold, then counting the balls when they have dropped out into the collection tube. If fewer than eight balls drop out, then one or more have caught on sand in the manifold.

Before Improvement:

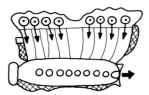

The eight balls were counted visually after the collection gate was opened manually. The balls were often miscounted, and residual sand caused trouble in subsequent processes.

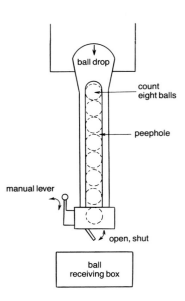

After Improvement:

A limit switch is used to check the number of balls as they line up in the collection tube. When the switch confirms that eight balls are present, the gate is opened automatically by an automatic plunger and the next operation is performed. If there are seven or fewer balls, a buzzer sounds and the next process cannot be performed.

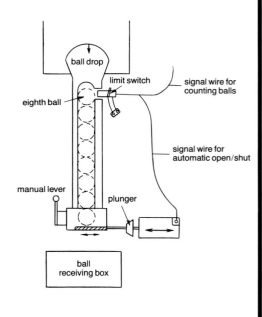

• *Example 33*

Process: Parts transport line	**Prevent Error:**	**Shutdown:**
Problem: Parts supplied upside down to automatic machinery	**Detect Error:** X	**Control:** X
Solution: Remove upside down parts with improved guide chute		**Alarm:**

Key Improvement: Chute modified to sort out defective parts

Description of Process: Processes before and after a pressing process are linked together by a transport device. In the next process the workpieces are mounted in place in the same position they arrive. Therefore, parts that arrive upside down at the pressing machine will be processed wrong or damage the machine.

Before Improvement:

Workers had to watch the incoming workpieces carefully and push improperly positioned items out of the line. Some upside down parts always got overlooked.

right side up

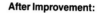
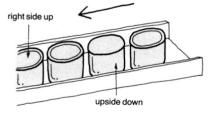

upside down

workpiece

After Improvement:

A checkpoint was installed in the delivery chute that automatically removes upside down items. The checkpoint has a notch that causes the upside down items to drop into the delivery box below. Those items that are right side up are allowed to pass through freely. As a result, all the workpieces are delivered to the next process in the proper positions.

right side up   upside down   right side up

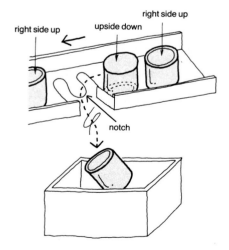

notch

● *Example 34*

Process: Machining forged shaft blanks

Problem: Incorrectly forged blanks

Solution: Out-of-tolerance blanks will not fit into jig

Key Improvement: Jig modified to detect defective parts

Prevent Error:

Detect Error: X

Shutdown:

Control:

Alarm:

Description of Process: Forged shaft blanks are machined to finished dimensions using a duplicator milling process.

Before Improvement:

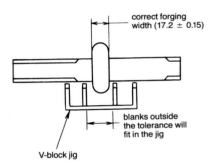

correct forging width (17.2 ± 0.15)

blanks outside the tolerance will fit in the jig

V-block jig

After the blanks were set in place in the jig, clamping the part with a vice actuated the processing by an interlocking circuit. Using forged blanks that were larger than dimensional tolerances led to imprecise finished dimensions due excessive tool contact that caused chipping.

After Improvement:

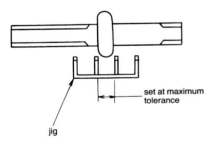

set at maximum tolerance

jig

The jig was made more precise. If a blank is not within dimensional tolerances, it will not fit the jig and cannot be processed. This makes it possible to discover imperfectly forged items before they are machined.

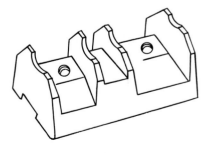

perspective view of jig

● *Example 35*

Process: Press-bending punched sheet metal

Problem: Part set up upside down

Solution: Change shape of part and jig

Key Improvement: Part and jig modified to guarantee correct positioning

Prevent Error: X

Detect Error:

Shutdown:

Control: X

Alarm:

Description of Process: A punched piece of sheet metal is positioned in a jig and bent in a press.

Before Improvement:

It was possible to place the piece in the jig incorrectly with the burr side up, so that the rough edges were on the wrong side of the bend.

workpiece

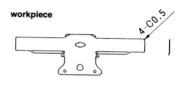

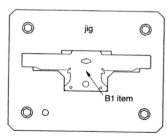

After Improvement:

The shape of the piece and the jig were altered slightly in a nonfunctional area so that the piece cannot be placed into the jig the wrong way.

workpiece

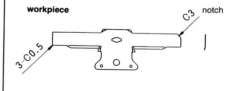

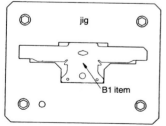

● *Example 36*

Process: Punching holes

Problem: Part set up upside down

Solution: Interference pin on jig

Key Improvement: Jig modified to guarantee correct positioning

Prevent Error: X

Detect Error:

Shutdown:

Control: X

Alarm:

Description of Process: A press is used to punch holes in a certain fitting.

Before Improvement:

It was possible to mount the fittings upside down on the jig. When the regular operator was absent, the substitute operators sometimes misread the drawing and processed the fittings upside down, resulting in a defective lot.

After Improvement:

An interference pin was installed on the jig. If the workpiece is mounted upside down, it strikes against the interference pin and does not fit properly. This makes it possible to identify mounting errors immediately.

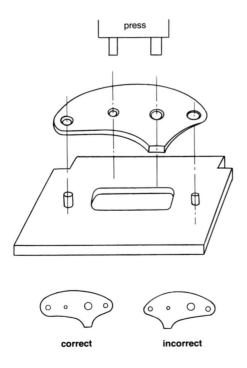

correct   incorrect

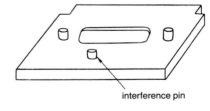

interference pin

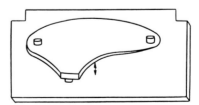

cannot be mounted upside down

● *Example 37*

Process: Tapping

Problem: Part mounted in jig upside down

Solution: Interference pin

Prevent Error: X

Detect Error:

Shutdown:

Control: X

Alarm:

Key Improvement: Jig modified to guarantee correct positioning

Description of Process: A workpiece is set into a jig and tapped for two screws. The part of the workpiece that fits into the jig has the same external shape and dimensions top and bottom. However, the internal depth on the A side (top) is less than the depth on the B side (bottom).

Before Improvement:

The jig allowed the workpiece to be mounted upside down, so the holes were drilled and threaded in the B side. These defects were discovered only during later assembly.

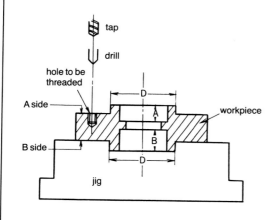

After Improvement:

Two interference pins were put into the processing jig. Now, if the workpiece is mounted upside down, there is a gap between the jig and the workpiece and it will not seat properly. The operator notices immediately that the workpiece is upside down. Inadvertent errors are eliminated.

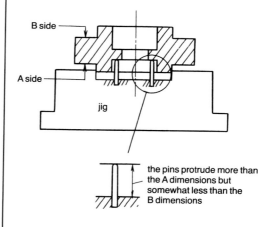

● *Example 38*

Process: Milling

Problem: Parts mounted in reverse

Solution: Improved jig

Key Improvement: Jig modified to guarantee correct positioning

Prevent Error: X

Detect Error:

Shutdown:

Control:

Alarm: X

Description of Process: In many cases, jigs continue in use without any change even after partial design changes have been made in the shapes of workpieces. In this case, the parts have symmetrical shapes with two notches on one side and one notch on the other side. In the past it did not matter which side had which notches. Then a design change was made, requiring the upper surface to be milled on the side where there was only one notch.

Before Improvement:

Correct operation depended on the vigilance of the operators. However, the operators frequently performed the milling without checking. As a result there were constant processing errors in which the upper surface was milled on the two-notch side.

After Improvement:

The jig was improved with the addition of a spring-mounted detecting pin. Now, if the workpiece is mistakenly mounted the wrong way, the pin is pressed down, actuating a limit switch and turning on a warning lamp. As a result the processing errors no longer occur.

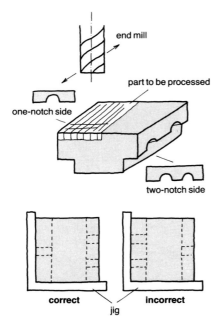

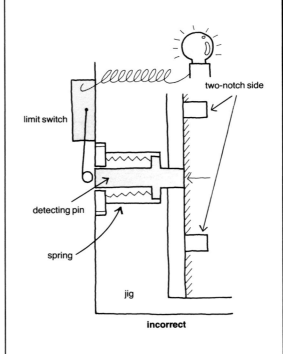

● *Example 39*

Process: Casting and molding products

Problem: Misshapen items

Solution: Testing collet used in final process to detect misshapen items

Key Improvement: Jig modified to detect defective parts

Prevent Error:

Detect Error: X

Shutdown:

Control: X

Alarm:

Description of Process: Items were produced by die casting or pressing and inspected for deformities.

Before Improvement:

Misshapen items produced in these processes were sometimes not discovered by simple visual inspection before products were delivered, which led to customer complaints.

nondefective

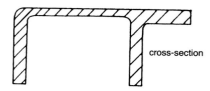

cross-section

defective

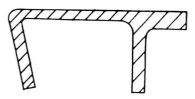

After Improvement:

A jig conforming exactly to the standard dimensions of the product is used in the final pressing process so that defective items cannot be set in place. This completely eliminates delivery of defective items.

nondefective

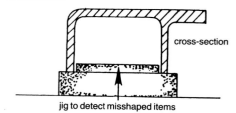

cross-section

jig to detect misshaped items

defective

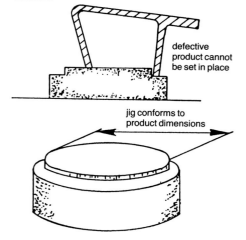

defective product cannot be set in place

jig conforms to product dimensions

● *Example 40*

Process: Press-fitting

Problem: Parts not pressed all the way

Solution: Gate on jig used to check for incomplete pressing

Key Improvement: Jig modified to detect defective parts

Prevent Error:

Detect Error: X

Shutdown:

Control: X

Alarm:

Description of Process: Part A is set in a jig and part B is pressed into the hole in part A.

Before Improvement:

Workers were supposed to inspect the parts to make sure that insertion was sufficient, but often insufficient insertion was overlooked due to carelessness of the operators.

After Improvement:

A gate was installed on the jig. If part B is not inserted sufficiently, it strikes against the gate, preventing the operator from removing the work-piece from the jig.

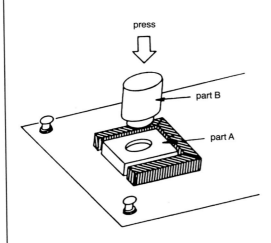

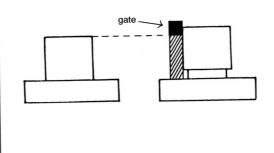

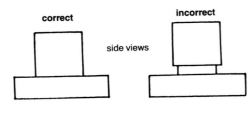

● *Example 41*

Process: Thimbles are shrink-fitted onto shafts

Problem: Protrusions on the shaft prevented proper seating

Solution: Shaft is tested with a gage before thimbles are mounted

Key Improvement: Gage used for inspection

Prevent Error: X

Detect Error:

Shutdown:

Control: X

Alarm:

Description of Process: Shrink-fitting is used to mount thimbles on shafts. The thimbles are removed from the heating furnace and pressed onto the shafts.

Before Improvement:

Troubles occurred when the thimbles did not fit properly because of dirt or protrusions on the shaft. If the thimbles could not be pressed on easily after heating, the operators beat them with a hammer, or used force to remove them and then polished the shafts with sandpaper. These techniques damaged the thimbles.

nondefective

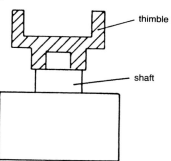

defective

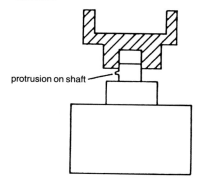

After Improvement:

A limit switch, a gage, and a photoelectric switch are used together to check that the shaft dimensions are correct before processing. When the shaft is properly in the jig, the limit switch turns on the photoelectric switch. If the gage fits the shaft normally, it interrupts the light and makes a visual signal indicating that the thimble will fit the shaft.

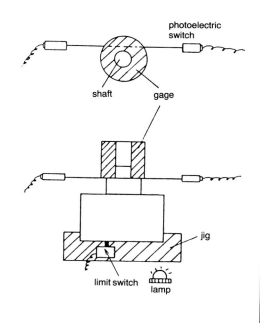

● *Example 42*

Process: Deburring injection molded parts

Problem: Deburring omitted

Solution: Detecting pin added to jig in subsequent process

Key Improvement: Jig modified to detect defective parts

Prevent Error:

Detect Error: X

Shutdown:

Control: X

Alarm:

Description of Process: If burrs are not removed after injection molding, the defect will not be discovered until the final inspection after final assembly.

Before Improvement:

The parts were deburred on the basis of visual inspection after injection molding, but operators sometimes missed defective parts.

nondefective

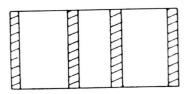

cross-section

defective

burrs

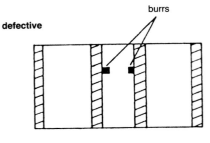

After Improvement:

A jig with a detecting pin is used in the next process. If the item is defective, the pin catches on the burr and the part cannot be set in position. Deburring errors are completely eliminated.

detecting pin

nondefective

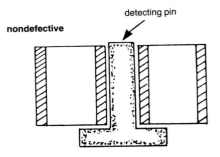

defective

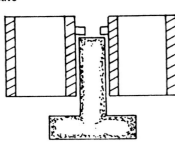

● *Example 43*

Process: Drilling

Problem: Holes not drilled to required depth

Solution: Limit switches detect start of drilling and proper depth

Key Improvement: Tool modified to guarantee correct processing

Prevent Error:

Detect Error: X

Shutdown:

Control:

Alarm: X

Description of Process: A series of holes are drilled in a plate.

Before Improvement:

The operator's skill was relied on to tell whether the hole was drilled to the correct depth. However, the drill was sometimes retracted before it had gone in all the way, resulting in faulty drilling. Troubles resulted during assembly.

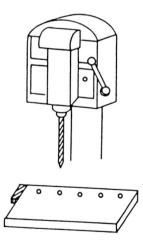

After Improvement:

Two limit switches were mounted on the drill press. Faulty drilling is indicated if limit switch 1 is released before limit switch 2 has been tripped. A buzzer is sounded to alert the operator.

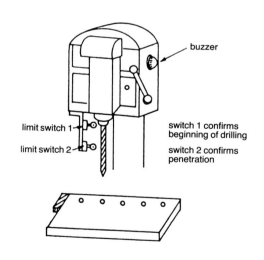

buzzer

limit switch 1

limit switch 2

switch 1 confirms beginning of drilling

switch 2 confirms penetration

● *Example 44*

Process: Soldering electric parts in motors

Problem: Solder bridges

Solution: Provide solder barriers in molded part

Key Improvement: Part modified to guarantee correct processing

Prevent Error: X

Detect Error:

Shutdown:

Control: X

Alarm:

Description of Process: Certain motor components have electrical leads soldered to five places on a molded insulator.

Before Improvement:

The spaces between the solder pads were narrow and solder bridges occurred if operators lacked skill or forgot to be careful.

After Improvement:

The insulator was improved (the molding dies are modified) to provide partitions between the solder pads. These act as barriers to the solder so it cannot run from one pad to the next. Solder bridges are completely eliminated.

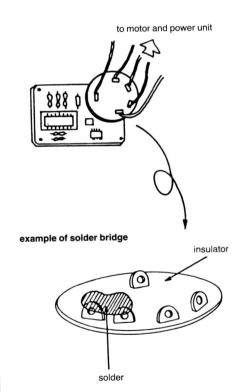

to motor and power unit

example of solder bridge

insulator

solder

insulator improved with barriers

● *Example 45*

Process: Drilling

Problem: Workpiece set in wrong position

Solution: Add pin to jig

Key Improvement: Jig modified to guarantee correct positioning

Prevent Error: X

Detect Error:

Shutdown:

Control: X

Alarm:

Description of Process: Workpieces have a set of holes punched by a turret punch press. They are then set up in a jig on a drill press, where more holes are drilled. It is easy to mistake the front of the workpiece for the back or the left side for the right side.

Before Improvement:

Workpieces were sometimes mounted in the drill press upside down or with right and left reversed, leading to holes drilled in the wrong place.

correctly mounted

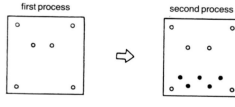

first process   second process

incorrectly mounted

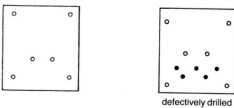

defectively drilled

After Improvement:

A pin corresponding to one of the holes punched in the previous process was mounted on the jig. Only when the piece is mounted properly will it fit into the jig for drilling.

correctly mounted

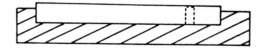

pin prevents incorrect mounting

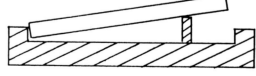

● *Example 46*

Process: Inspection of tapered item

Problem: Unbeveled items not detected

Solution: Improve gage to detect beveling

Key Improvement: Gage modified to test part

Prevent Error:

Detect Error: X

Shutdown:

Control: X

Alarm:

Description of Process: The taper on a certain machined part is inspected with a gage cut to the shape of the part. The part is supposed to have a beveled edge at the bottom of the taper.

Before Improvement:

The gage measured only the dimensions of the part and did not check for items that had not been beveled. Unbeveled items were not detected.

After Improvement:

The shape of the gage was improved so that it checks for beveling as well as measures the dimensions.

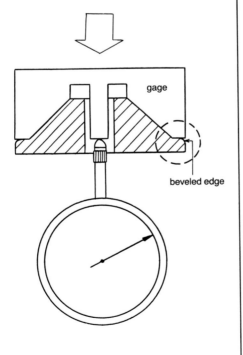

beveled edge

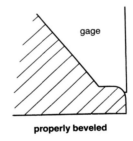

gage

properly beveled

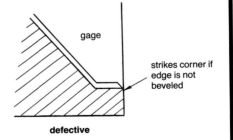

gage

strikes corner if edge is not beveled

defective

● *Example 47*

Process: Drilling tap holes in tubes

Problem: Tubes not positioned correctly

Solution: Additional guide on jig

Key Improvement: Jig modified to guarantee correct positioning

Prevent Error: X

Detect Error:

Shutdown:

Control: X

Alarm:

Description of Process: Cylinder tubes are set into a jig on a drill press and clamped in place against a target so holes can be drilled in the tap seats.

Before Improvement:

Although there was one positioning clamp on the jig, it was possible to clamp the workpiece so the tube was out of position, resulting in hole misalignment and eccentric holes.

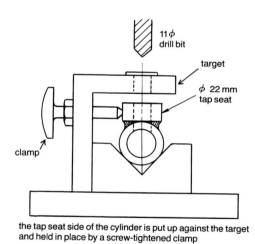

the tap seat side of the cylinder is put up against the target and held in place by a screw-tightened clamp

After Improvement:

A second clamp was provided to prevent incorrect positioning of the workpiece. This regulates alignment of the workpiece and completely eliminates defects.

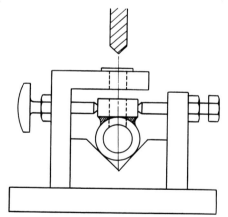

a second clamp is installed to prevent misalignment

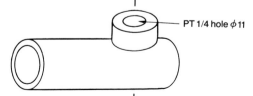

● *Example 48*

Process: Multispindle drilling

Problem: Setting workpiece in jig in wrong position

Solution: Additional guide blocks in jig

Key Improvement: Jig modified to guarantee correct positioning

Prevent Error: X

Detect Error:

Shutdown:

Control: X

Alarm:

Description of Process: Holes are drilled in the flanges of workpieces using a multispindle drill press.

Before Improvement:

It was possible to mount the workpiece in the jig in the wrong position. Defects resulted when holes were drilled in incorrect positions.

After Improvement:

Three guide blocks were added to the existing jig, improving it so it is impossible to mount the workpiece in the wrong position.

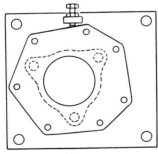

improper position

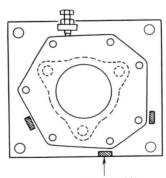

additional guides

7 drill holes, ϕ 9 mm
PCD 148 mm
length 181

● *Example 49*

Process: Tapping

Problem: Tapping depth not sufficient

Solution: Microswitch for detecting tap penetration

Key Improvement: Jig modified to guarantee correct processing

Prevent Error:

Detect Error: X

Shutdown:

Control:

Alarm: X

Description of Process: Holes are drilled and tapped in aluminum caging materials.

Before Improvement:

    Tapping was checked with a screw gage after the holes were threaded. However, items with insufficient tapping depth often resulted due to errors in setting the tap.

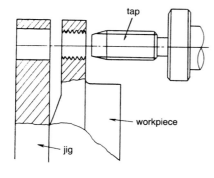

After Improvement:

    A microswitch for checking tap penetration was installed on the jig. Tap breakage and errors in setting the tap are both detected by this means.

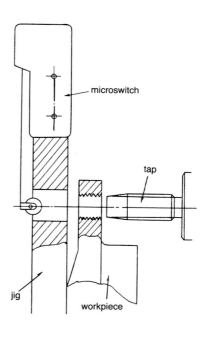

● *Example 50*

Process: Automatic parts feeder

Problem: Parts flipping upside down

Solution: Improve automatic shutters

Key Improvement: Chute modified to guarantee correct positioning

Prevent Error: X

Detect Error:

Shutdown:

Control: X

Alarm:

Description of Process: Parts are fed individually by an automatic feeder to a process for cutting grooves on shafts.

Before Improvement:

The shutters for individual feed on the shaft chutes were poorly designed and shafts in the chutes sometimes flipped upside down due to impact with the shutter. The grooves were then cut in the wrong end of the part, and no grooves were cut where they were needed.

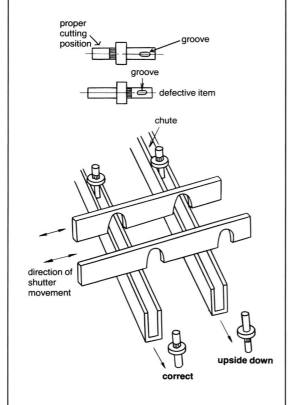

After Improvement:

The shutters were redesigned to move the shafts gently down the chute, preventing them from flipping due to impact.

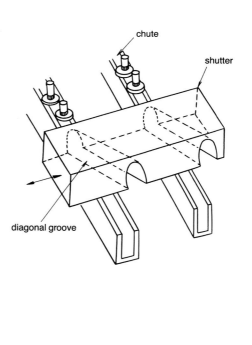

● *Example 51*

Process: Machining

Problem: Hand-held parts nicked during machining or machined while not centered

Solution: Jig to eliminate hand-held machining

Key Improvement: Jig used to guarantee correct processing

Prevent Error: X

Detect Error:

Shutdown:

Control: X

Alarm:

Description of Process: Shafts are finished on a machine.

Before Improvement:

Workers held the shafts in their bare hands to process them. This required skill and time because the workpieces were unstable and difficult to center. In addition, the hand-held shafts were likely to be hit and nicked.

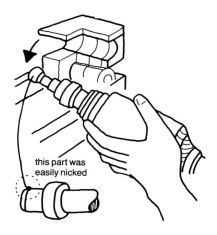

this part was easily nicked

After Improvement:

Holding platforms were devised for resting the workpieces. The jig and the shafts can be centered quickly and accurately, avoiding damage to the parts.

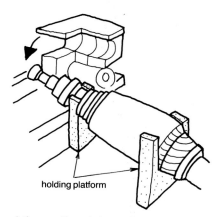

holding platform

platform positions shaft securely for machining

● Example 52

Process: Oxyacetylene cutting of large spherical sheets

Problem: Badly cut edges

Solution: Automate positioning of sheets being cut

Key Improvement: Jig modified to guarantee correct positioning

Prevent Error: X

Detect Error:

Shutdown:

Control: X

Alarm:

Description of Process: Large curved sheets of steel are cut with an automatic oxyacetylene torch in preparation for building tanks. The sheets are set into see-saw racks that move as the cutting is performed so the cutting torch remains horizontal.

Before Improvement:

The worker operated the hoist for the see-saw rack manually in time with the movement of the cutting torch so the torch was continuously horizontal. However, one operator was in charge of a number of units, and if he was careless or got behind, the racks were moved late or not at all, resulting in faulty cutting and bad edges.

After Improvement:

A timer was incorporated in the rack hoist to synchronize the speed of the automatic cutting torch with the speed of the hoist, so the cutter is always horizontal. This makes it possible to feed the cutter automatically and ensures good cutting results.

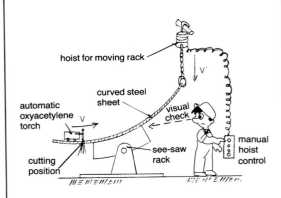

correctly cut

smooth edge — no gas notching

defective

rough edge — gas notching occurred

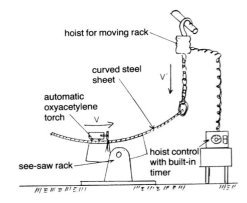

● *Example 53*

Process: Cutting raw material, with gravity feed device **Prevent Error:** X **Shutdown:** X

Problem: Positioning problems **Detect Error:** **Control:**

Solution: Install limit switch to detect proper positioning **Alarm:** X

Key Improvement: Operation prevented if part is not positioned correctly

Description of Process: A simplified automatic cutting machine is used to cut workpieces from raw materials. The raw material is fed by gravity, strikes a contact jig, and is cut by a gas cutting torch.

Before Improvement:

As more and more of the raw material was cut off, the supply became lighter and lighter until it became too light to position itself against the contact accurately. Defects occurred as a result.

After Improvement:

A proximity switch mounted inside the contact jig controls the device so the cutter will operate only after the switch indicates the workpiece is accurately set in place against the contact. A flashing light notifies the operator if the workpiece is improperly positioned.

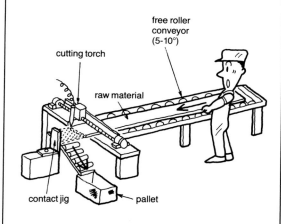

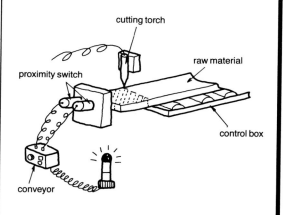

● *Example 54*

Process: Transporting tall, narrow pins on a conveyor belt

Problem: Pins tipped at junctions in the conveyor belt

Solution: Change positions of stabilizing devices

Key Improvement: Transport modified to guarantee correct positioning

Prevent Error: X

Detect Error:

Shutdown:

Control: X

Alarm:

Description of Process: Tall, narrow pins are transported on a conveyor belt.

Before Improvement:

After the diameter of the pins was reduced 10 percent and the speed of the conveyor was increased by 30 to 40 percent, the rate of pins tipping at junction points rose suddenly.

After Improvement:

After considering the dynamics carefully, starting from the static state, it was determined that the geometry of the stabilizing devices must be improved. The guide for keeping the pin vertical as it moves around curves was raised nearer the center of gravity of the pin, and the upper guide rail was raised above the center of gravity. These modifications improve the traveling stability of the pins and completely eliminate defects.

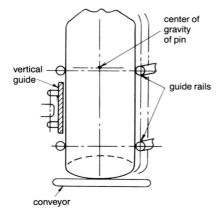

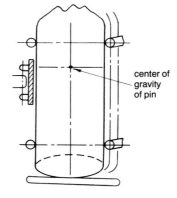

● *Example 55*

Process: Inspecting cassette tape decks

Problem: Inspection tapes out of sequence

Solution: Use "first-in, first-out" tape rack

Key Improvement: Tool modified to guarantee correct processing

Prevent Error: X

Detect Error:

Shutdown:

Control: X

Alarm:

Description of Process: When a cassette deck is inspected, the inspector uses a series of cassette tapes to check the performance of the unit. It is important that the inspector perform the tests in the proper sequence and that all the tests are performed.

Before Improvement:

A slotted rack was used to store the tapes. If a tape was accidentally placed on the worktable or carried off, the inspector could lose track of how far inspection had gone. Errors might occur because the inspector thought that inspections had been performed that had not.

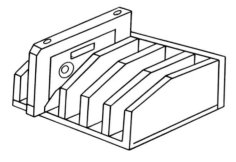

After Improvement:

A new "first-in, first-out" rack was developed that dispenses the tapes only in the proper order for testing. When one tape is removed for use, the next tape slides down, ready for use. When a tape has been used, the inspector places it in the top of the rack, where it remains in the correct order. Errors in the testing sequence are completely eliminated.

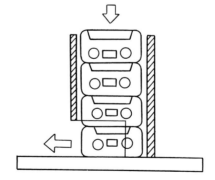

● *Example 56*

Process: Countersinking

Problem: Parts countersunk on wrong side

Solution: Prevent errors with new jig

Key Improvement: Jig modified to guarantee correct positioning

Prevent Error: X

Detect Error:

Shutdown:

Control: X

Alarm:

Description of Process: A screw hole on a small part is countersunk.

Before Improvement:

It was possible to set the part on the drill press table upside down and countersink the wrong side.

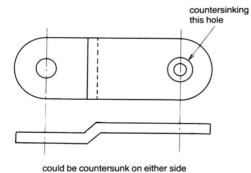

could be countersunk on either side

countersinking this hole

After Improvement:

A new jig was designed with a poka-yoke pin that prevents the part from being set up upside down. Reverse countersinking is completely eliminated.

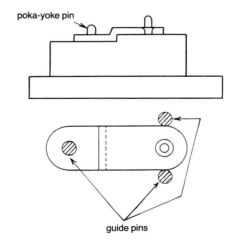

poka-yoke pin

guide pins

Assembly Errors

● *Example 57*

Process: Tightening nuts

Problem: Missing washers

Solution: Modify nut driver so nuts can't be tightened if washer is missing

Key Improvement: Tool modified to guarantee correct processing

Prevent Error: X

Detect Error:

Shutdown:

Control: X

Alarm:

Description of Process: Nuts were tightened using an automatic nut driver.

Before Improvement:

It was possible to tighten the nuts even if their washers were missing, and checking for the washers relied on worker vigilance. Defects occurred when nuts were tightened with their washers missing.

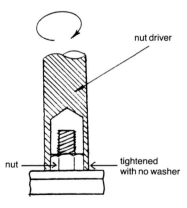

After Improvement:

A stopper was built into the nut driver. If the washer is missing, the bolt strikes the stopper and prevents the driver from tightening the nut. Missing washers are completely eliminated. Note: For this poka-yoke to work, variations in length of the bolt must be very carefully controlled.

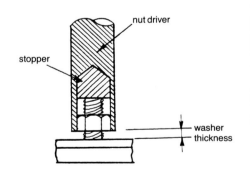

● *Example 58*

Process: Changing setup of molding dies with separate bridges

Problem: Faulty bridge placement

Solution: Change shape of die body

Prevent Error: X

Detect Error:

Shutdown:

Control: X

Alarm:

Key Improvement: Tool modified to guarantee correct processing

Description of Process: In molding operations, bridges are replaced to alter the die shape for different models.

Before Improvement:

Because the bridges were symmetrical right to left, they were sometimes mounted in reverse by inexperienced operators, leading to defects.

After Improvement:

The shape of the bridge was altered to prevent reverse mounting. Defects due to faulty placement of bridges are completely eliminated.

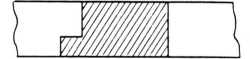

body of die

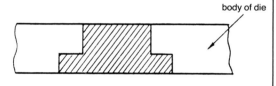

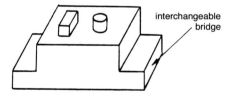

interchangeable bridge

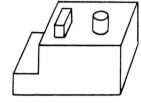

● *Example 59*

Process: Mounting variable capacitors to circuit boards

Problem: Breakage of top-mounted terminals

Solution: Change connection method

Key Improvement: Part modified to protect it from damage

Prevent Error: X

Detect Error:

Shutdown:

Control: X

Alarm:

Description of Process: Variable capacitors (with attached potentiometers) are mounted onto circuit boards. The potentiometer terminal is located at the top of the capacitor, and it is important to prevent other items from touching the terminal.

Before Improvement:

Plastic tubing was glued over the terminal connection to prevent other items from touching it. However, force had to be applied to the terminal to attach the tubing, and the terminal sometimes broke under the pressure.

After Improvement:

A new method of attaching and insulating the terminal was developed. Additional work becomes unnecessary, and the defects caused by the tubing are completely eliminated. The standard time for assembly is also reduced.

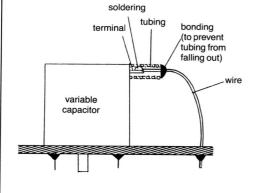

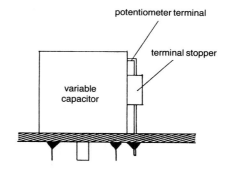

● *Example 60*

Process: Assembly of control units of cassette decks

Problem: Order of items was confused

Solution: Group items as one part until after assembly

Key Improvement: Part modified to guarantee correct positioning

Prevent Error: X

Detect Error:

Shutdown:

Control: X

Alarm:

Description of Process: The levers for control units of cassette decks are assembled.

Before Improvement:

Levers A, B, C, and D were each assembled separately. It was difficult to differentiate these parts without paying considerable attention, and defects occurred when parts were confused.

After Improvement:

The four levers that were confused when handled separately are now grouped together. The levers are combined into one unit by means of a coupling part. After assembly into the tape deck, the coupling part is broken off. Assembly errors are completely eliminated. Only one part number is needed and the number of managerial workhours has been reduced.

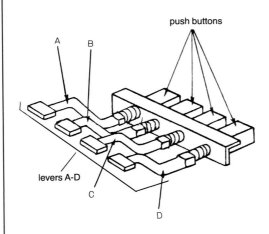

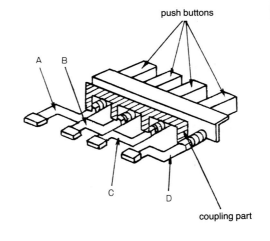

● *Example 61*

Process: Mounting cases on thick film hybrid ICs

Problem: Cases mounted backwards

Solution: Interference pin designed into case

Key Improvement: Part modified to guarantee correct positioning

Prevent Error: X

Detect Error:

Shutdown:

Control: X

Alarm:

Description of Process: Cases are mounted onto thick-film hybrid ICs.

Before Improvement:

It was difficult to tell from the outer appearance of the case which direction the case was to be mounted.

After Improvement:

A boss was designed into the inside of the case as an interference pin to prevent the case from being mounted in reverse. Defects due to mounting the case wrong are completely eliminated, and 100 percent accuracy in mounting the cases is achieved.

boss strikes a part
on the IC if case
is mounted backwards

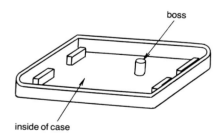

boss

inside of case

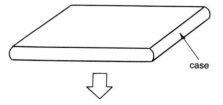

case

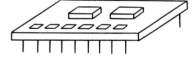

● *Example 62*

Process: Mounting LEDs on circuit boards

Problem: LEDs mounted backwards, resulting in faulty polarity

Solution: Modify contacts to correspond to different lengths of anode and cathode

Key Improvement: Part modified to guarantee correct positioning

Prevent Error: X

Detect Error:

Shutdown:

Control: X

Alarm:

Description of Process: LEDs are assembled on the display of an electronic measuring device.

Before Improvement:

LEDs were often assembled with anode and cathode reversed.

After Improvement:

The defect phenomena were analyzed and the shape of the parts was used to develop the improvement. The anode and cathode terminals of the LEDs have different lengths. Therefore, the length of the LED contacts is matched with the length of the terminals, making it impossible to fully insert the LEDs to the stopper position if they are inserted in reverse. Defects due to reverse mounting of LEDs are completely eliminated.

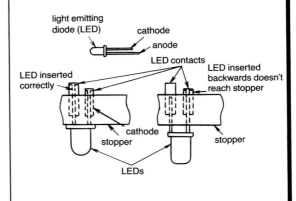

● *Example 63*

Process: Mounting circuit boards into assemblies   **Prevent Error:**   **Shutdown:**

Problem: Missing mounting holes in circuit boards   **Detect Error:** X   **Control:** X

Solution: Detecting pins installed in circuit board inspection step   **Alarm:**

Key Improvement: Jig modified to detect defective parts

Description of Process: Circuit boards are inspected, then later mounted into assemblies.

Before Improvement:

Sometimes circuit boards could not be mounted into their assemblies because screw holes had not been drilled in them. The workers in earlier processes relied on visual checks to determine whether screw holes had been drilled.

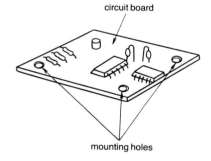

circuit board

mounting holes

After Improvement:

Detecting pins were installed on the jig used for checking the circuit boards after wiring. Circuit boards without the proper holes cannot be mounted on the jig. All circuit boards that lack mounting holes are now detected before they are sent on to assembly.

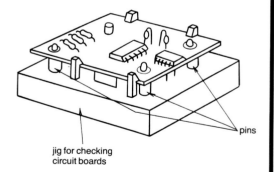

pins

jig for checking circuit boards

● *Example 64*

Process: Press-fitting shafts

Problem: Shaft scratched due to improper insertion into jig

Solution: Use magnet to position shaft

Prevent Error: X

Detect Error:

Shutdown:

Control: X

Alarm:

Key Improvement: Jig modified to guarantee correct positioning

Description of Process: Shafts are inserted into a receiving jig for press-fitting.

Before Improvement:

If the shaft was not inserted straight into the receiving jig, the shaft scraped against the jig and was scratched.

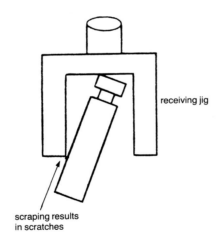

receiving jig

scraping results in scratches

After Improvement:

A magnet was mounted to ensure that the shaft is inserted in the jig in a perpendicular position. Scratching is completely eliminated.

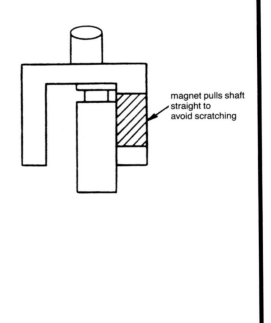

magnet pulls shaft straight to avoid scratching

● *Example 65*

Process: Processing a variety of materials of different sizes

Problem: Positioning and setup errors

Solution: Use one setup for all items

Key Improvement: Part and jig modified to guarantee correct positioning

Prevent Error: X

Detect Error:

Shutdown:

Control: X

Alarm:

Description of Process: A number of different sizes of plates are processed using one jig.

Before Improvement:

The edges of the plates were used as positioning references. Reference positioning had to be redone for each different size, and setup errors resulted.

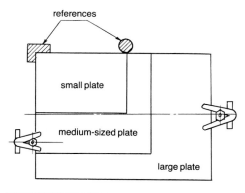

upper edge was used as a positioning reference

After Improvement:

The process and materials were modified so that only one setup is needed for all the plates, regardless of their sizes. Locator pins built into the jig correspond to double holes drilled in the center of every plate so that all sizes of plates are automatically positioned correctly by merely setting them on the jig. Processing errors are completely eliminated.

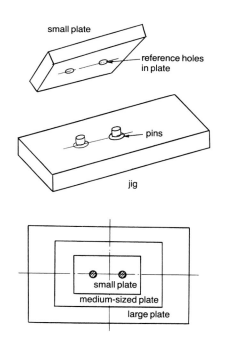

● *Example 66*

Process: Camera assembly

Problem: Camera bodies and back lids matched incorrectly

Solution: Add assembly check into automatic focusing check

Key Improvement: Tool modified to make additional test

Prevent Error:

Detect Error: X

Shutdown:

Control:

Alarm: X

Description of Process: In a camera assembly process, camera lids are attached to the main camera bodies. Sometimes a back lid with dating functions is attached to a regular unit, or a regular back lid is attached to a body with dating functions.

Before Improvement:

The workers in a subsequent process made visual checks to see whether the cameras were assembled with the correct bodies and lids and rejected those that did not match. The checks depended entirely on the workers' vigilance. Inadvertent errors resulted and some defective units moved along the line.

After Improvement:

Since the process of mounting the back lids is combined with the process of checking the automatic focusing, the automatic focusing device was improved so the shutter does not operate during the check if there are lid assembly mistakes. This makes it possible to detect mismatched lids perfectly during the mounting process.

	Body	Back lid	Pass/Fail	Switch		Shutter
1	regular body	regular lid	○	body OFF	back lid OFF	release
2	regular body	dating function lid	×	OFF	ON	can't release
3	dating function body	regular lid	×	ON	OFF	can't release
4	dating function body	dating function lid	○	ON	ON	release

If the main unit and the back lid are assembled correctly, the switch goes on, the shutter works, and the unit moves on without any problem. If the shutter does not work, it means the unit has been incorrectly assembled, and the unit does not move on to the subsequent processes.

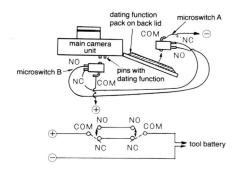

● *Example 67*

Process: Assembly line

Problem: Wrong parts used

Solution: Automatic parts box

Key Improvement: Selection of parts automated

Prevent Error: X

Detect Error:

Shutdown:

Control: X

Alarm:

Description of Process: A number of different small parts are stored beside the assembly line to shorten the time required when changing over from one model to another.

Before Improvement:

The parts were all kept in open boxes along the line, and sometimes the parts were confused and mismatched.

After Improvement:

The storage boxes for the parts were improved so that only the parts needed for a particular model can be taken out. A limit switch is mounted on the line to detect automatically the car model currently being assembled. A device actuated by the limit switch covers the boxes that are not in current use. This eliminates mismatching of small parts.

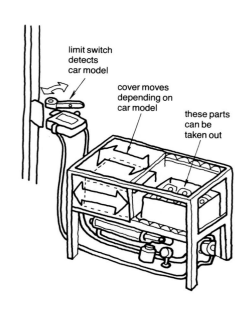

limit switch detects car model

cover moves depending on car model

these parts can be taken out

● *Example 68*

Process: Testing plastics

Problem: Setup errors on testing machine

Solution: Setup templates for each type of plastic tested

Key Improvement: Gage used for inspection

Prevent Error: X

Detect Error:

Shutdown:

Control: X

Alarm:

Description of Process: A number of different types of plastic batches are tested using a testing machine. It is necessary to set up the conditions, such as temperature, time, and pressure, differently for each type of plastic.

Before Improvement:

Errors sometimes occurred when the operators misread the scales or the instruction documents. Therefore, deviations sometimes occurred in the tests, and it was often necessary to repeat the tests to confirm the results.

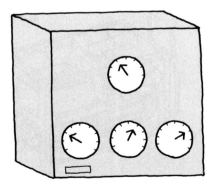

After Improvement:

Transparent templates for setting the conditions were prepared for each different type of plastic. When beginning operations, the operator first checks the type of plastic to be tested, then takes the appropriate template out of the case and attaches it to the instrument panel. The template is marked with the correct settings for each of the dials and instruments on the instrument panel, ensuring that testing is done according to the proper procedures.

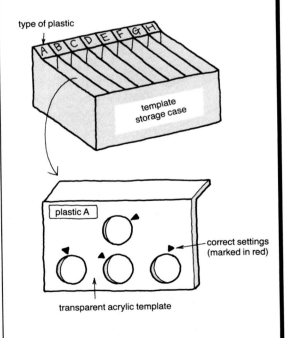

type of plastic

A B C D E F G H

template storage case

plastic A

correct settings (marked in red)

transparent acrylic template

● *Example 69*

Process: Mounting valve spools onto a casing

Problem: Parts were mounted reversed end to end

Solution: Improved storage rack

Key Improvement: Jig modified to guarantee correct positioning

Prevent Error: X

Detect Error:

Shutdown:

Control: X

Alarm:

Description of Process: Valve spools are mounted onto casings. There is a difference of 1 mm between the A dimension and the B dimension that cannot be distinguished by visual inspection.

Before Improvement:

The parts arrived in boxes with some parts aligned in the A direction and some aligned in the B direction. Each spool was checked with calipers, but in some cases the parts were inadvertently assembled in the wrong direction.

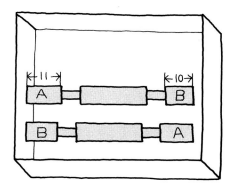

After Improvement:

A special rack that automatically distinguishes between the different dimensions was designed for laying out the parts. The parts fit only in one direction, which makes it unnecessary to measure them with calipers before assembling. There is no longer any need to check them carefully. This process also serves as an inspection process, detecting grooves cut in the wrong positions in the preceding processes.

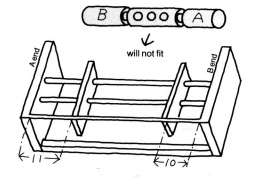

● *Example 70*

Process: Assembly line

Problem: Commonly used parts out of stock

Solution: Automatic parts bin with low stock detectors

Key Improvement: Bin modified to test itself

Prevent Error: X

Detect Error:

Shutdown:

Control: X

Alarm:

Description of Process: Everyone is always careful to ensure a constant stock of special parts needed in assembling, but supplies used in common and general-purpose supplies tend to be overlooked. However, these are necessary parts for assembling, and work will stop without them.

Before Improvement:

Different sizes of straight pins and tapered pins are used in a workplace. The pins are arranged by size and stored in a cabinet, from which they are taken when needed. Sometimes certain pins were out of stock, and this held up assembly. In addition, the pins at the bottoms of the drawers had been lying there a long time and they sometimes became rusty. Stocking the pins was neglected because there was no particular person who monitored the stock.

After Improvement:

A storage cabinet was built, with boxes containing various sizes and shapes of pins. Each box is equipped with a switch that detects when the pins are in low supply and lights a red lamp for that box on the display panel. This makes it possible to notify the acquisitions department immediately, eliminating the rush and confusion that was the rule in the past.

New pins are put in the boxes from the back and pins are taken out from the front. This "first-in, first-out" arrangement makes it possible to avoid backlogs of old pins remaining a long time and rusting.

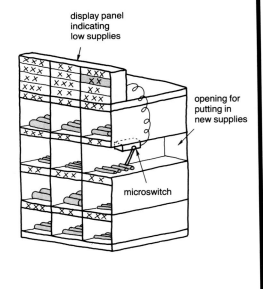

display panel indicating low supplies

opening for putting in new supplies

microswitch

● *Example 71*

Process: Mounting brackets

Problem: Brackets mounted in the wrong direction

Solution: Detector to prevent further processing when brackets mounted backwards

Key Improvement: Jig modified to detect defective parts

Prevent Error:

Detect Error: X

Shutdown:

Control: X

Alarm:

Description of Process: Brackets were spot-welded to bars.

Before Improvement:

The brackets were sometimes attached to the bars backwards. If these pieces were not detected, they would be assembled, leading to defects that had to be reworked later.

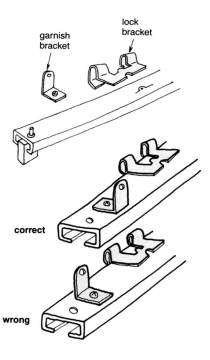

After Improvement:

A poka-yoke angle iron was installed on the jig for the next process to detect bars with brackets mounted backwards by keeping them from seating on the jig.

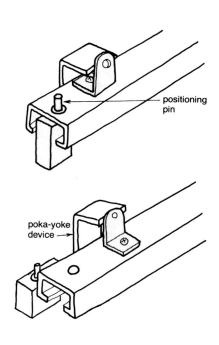

● *Example 72*

Process: Mounting front floor for right-hand steering cars

Problem: Front floor for left-hand steering mounted

Solution: Modify jig to prevent mismatched mounting

Key Improvement: Jig modified to guarantee correct processing

Prevent Error: X

Detect Error:

Shutdown:

Control: X

Alarm:

Description of Process: Front floors are mounted on automobile chassis. Different floors are used for cars with right-hand and left-hand steering mechanisms.

Before Improvement:

A model meant to be made with left-hand steering was sometimes constructed with a front floor meant for a right-hand steering car.

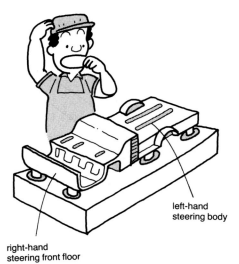

right-hand
steering front floor

left-hand
steering body

After Improvement:

A limit switch in the floor-mounting area detects the arrival of a left-hand steering car. This raises a pin mounted on an air cylinder in the position of the left-hand steering column hole. When the pin is raised, only a left-hand floor can be mounted on the chassis.

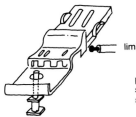

limit switch

positioning pin rises when limit switch hits step on left-hand steering car

air cylinder

correct
pin passes through steering column hole

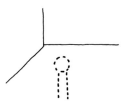

wrong
front floor for right-hand steering cannot be mounted over pin

● *Example 73*

Process:	Inserting circuit boards into backplates	**Prevent Error:**	X	**Shutdown:**	
Problem:	Detection circuit boards and control circuit board were confused	**Detect Error:**		**Control:**	X
Solution:	Guide pins matching unique notches in each circuit board			**Alarm:**	

Key Improvement: Part modified to guarantee correct positioning

---

Description of Process: Circuit boards for two different circuits were plugged into backplates in an electronic device.

Before Improvement:

The circuit boards for the detection circuit and the control circuit had identical connecting pins and their appearance and specifications were similar. Therefore, mistakes occurred when they were interchanged accidentally, and errors were detectable only after final assembly.

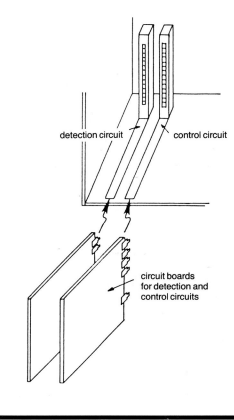

After Improvement:

A distinct guide is attached to each backplate and corresponding notches are made on each of the circuit boards to prevent mixups in assembly.

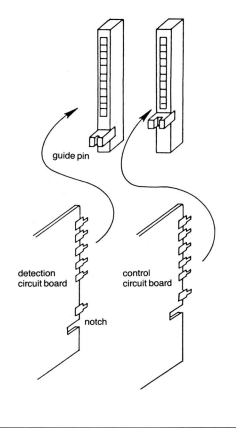

● *Example 74*

Process: Tightening nuts

Problem: Insufficient torque caused by drops in pneumatic pressure

Solution: Air pressure sensor

Key Improvement: Operation tied to value of critical physical quantity

Prevent Error:

Detect Error: X

Shutdown: X

Control:

Alarm: X

Description of Process: Nuts are tightened with a specified torque with a power wrench driven by pneumatic pressure supplied throughout the factory.

Before Improvement:

If air pressure dropped during tightening, no warning of the problem was given, and the conveyor continued to move. Therefore, bolts were tightened with insufficient torque.

After Improvement:

An air pressure meter was installed in the air line. A lamp blinks, an alarm rings, and the conveyor stops if the air pressure drops below a critical point.

● *Example 75*

Process: Pressing

Problem: Workpieces not set into die correctly

Solution: Limit switch to detect proper setup

Key Improvement: Jig modified to guarantee correct positioning

Prevent Error: X

Detect Error:

Shutdown: X

Control:

Alarm:

Description of Process: Products are set into a die and pressed.

Before Improvement:

    The operator checked that the products were in place before pressing. However, many defects resulted from errors when setting up the workpieces.

After Improvement:

    A limit switch is used to make sure the press cannot be activated unless the product is set in place perfectly. As a result, defects caused by errors when setting up the products are completely eliminated.

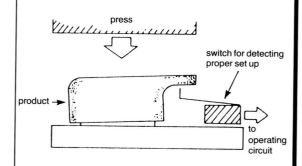

● *Example 76*

Process: Drilling holes in a side plate

Problem: Workpiece set up upside down or reversed

Solution: Limit switch detects asymmetrical features of workpiece

Key Improvement: Jig modified to guarantee correct positioning

Prevent Error: X

Detect Error:

Shutdown: X

Control:

Alarm:

Description of Process: A workpiece, a side plate, is set into position on a drill press and dowel holes are drilled. The workpiece is essentially symmetrical, and back and front are difficult to distinguish at a glance, although two edges are grooved along their length.

Before Improvement:

The workers, when setting the workpiece into position, checked to see whether the top and bottom of the plate were in the correct position. They then drilled the dowel holes. Inexperienced workers sometimes confused top for bottom and drilled the holes in the wrong places. Even veteran workers sometimes mounted the part backwards. These defects were discovered only at assembly.

After Improvement:

The grooved edges of two sides of the workpieces are used as guides for setting up the plates correctly. A limit switch is mounted on the jig and interlocked with the start switch so it is impossible to start the drill press if the side plate is set in the wrong position. Defects due to defective holes are completely eliminated.

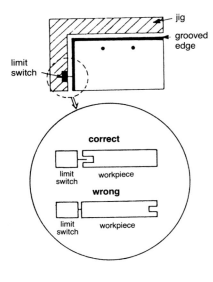

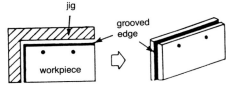

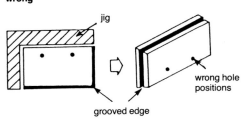

● *Example 77*

Process: Mounting brackets on cases

Problem: Cases set in jig upside down

Solution: Additional guide on jig to prevent upside down setup

Key Improvement: Jig modified to guarantee correct positioning

Prevent Error: X

Detect Error:

Shutdown:

Control: X

Alarm:

Description of Process: Brackets are mounted on cases that are more or less symmetrical on top and bottom except for a notch on the bottom.

Before Improvement:

The cases were supposed to be inserted in the jigs with the notched side down. However, the operator sometimes mistakenly put the cases in position upside down before mounting the bracket, resulting in a defective product.

correct

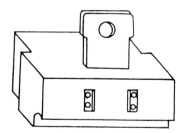

defective

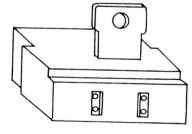

After Improvement:

A guide was mounted on the jig so the cases do not fit in place upside down. This completely eliminated mounting errors.

correct

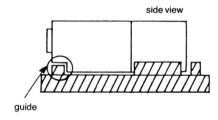

side view

guide

upside down

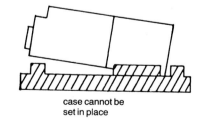

case cannot be
set in place

● *Example 78*

Process: Drilling

Problem: Workpieces set up backwards

Solution: Additional pin on jig

Key Improvement: Jig modified to guarantee correct positioning

Prevent Error: X

Detect Error:

Shutdown:

Control: X

Alarm:

Description of Process: The workpiece is set into the jig and drilled. The workpiece has two cutouts on the underside.

Before Improvement:

Even when the workers in charge were attentive, it frequently happened that the workpieces were set in position and drilled backwards, resulting in defects because the holes were in the wrong position.

After Improvement:

An interference pin was mounted on the jig to fit into one of the cutouts on the bottom. If a workpiece is set in place backwards, the workpiece sticks up and cannot be drilled. The errors ceased completely after this pin was mounted.

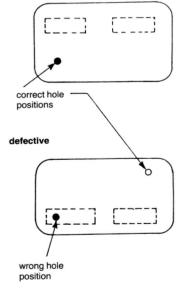

correct

correct hole positions

defective

wrong hole position

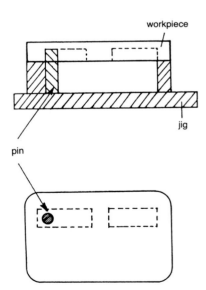

workpiece

jig

pin

● *Example 79*

Process: Press-fitting a curved pipe

Problem: Wrong end of curved pipe inserted in jig

Solution: Detect correct fit using vacuum gauge

Prevent Error:

Detect Error: X

Shutdown: X

Control:

Alarm:

Key Improvement: Operation prevented if part is not positioned correctly

---

Description of Process: Curved pipes are press-fitted using a jig, in which they are inserted. The pipes appear symmetrical, but one end is a little longer than the other. The longer end is beveled, and is the correct end to insert in the jig.

Before Improvement:

The procedure was to bevel the pipes, then check the beveling visually to determine which end to insert in the jig. However, the difference in length is only 2 mm, and it was possible to insert the pipe backwards. Sometimes the pipes were press-fitted backwards, resulting in defects.

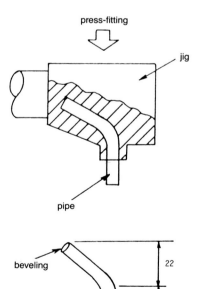

After Improvement:

If a pipe is mounted in reverse, there is a clearance between the pipe and the jig. A vacuum gauge was installed at this clearance and interlocked with the press power circuit. If the pipe is mounted in reverse, there is no vacuum and it is impossible to switch on the press. Defects are completely eliminated with this measure.

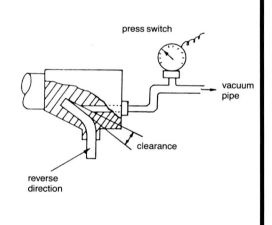

● *Example 80*

Process: Assembling tilted lock links

Problem: Links assembled using wrong hole

Solution: Use jig with guide pins to position

Key Improvement: Jig used to guarantee correct positioning

Prevent Error: X

Detect Error:

Shutdown:

Control: X

Alarm:

Description of Process: Lot side plates were attached to tilted lock links using a rivet and a spacer.

Before Improvement:

It was possible to attach the lot side plate to the wrong hole on the tilted lock link.

After Improvement:

A jig with reference pins for the main hook assembling hole and the edge was devised to hold the tilted lock link in the proper position for assembly. It is impossible to seat the piece on the jig if it is turned the wrong way.

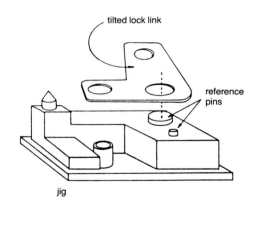

● *Example 81*

Process: Bending

Problem: Workpieces mounted upside down in bending jig

Solution: Guide pins in jig

Key Improvement: Jig modified to guarantee correct positioning

Prevent Error: X

Detect Error:

Shutdown:

Control: X

Alarm:

Description of Process: A plate with holes at diagonal corners is bent by a press.

Before Improvement:

The worker checked the orientation of the work-piece before setting it in the jig. However, the workpieces were sometimes processed upside down. The defects were discovered only at assembly, causing delays in delivery.

correct

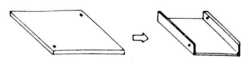

defective

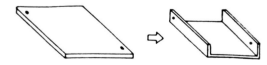

After Improvement:

Two pins were mounted in the jig making it impossible to set up the workpiece upside down. This scheme eliminates defective items.

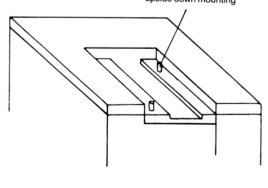

pin to prevent upside down mounting

● *Example 82*

Process: Tapping

Problem: Workpiece set up incorrectly

Solution: Improve jig

Key Improvement: Jig modified to guarantee correct positioning

Prevent Error: X

Detect Error:

Shutdown:

Control: X

Alarm:

Description of Process: Threads are cut in specified places in a workpiece placed in a jig.

Before Improvement:

Workpieces were sometimes set in the jig incorrectly without the operator noticing. The operator produced defective items when this happened.

After Improvement:

The jig was remodeled and an interference plate was mounted to ensure that the workpiece is set in the correct position even if the operator is not paying careful attention. The backing guide was made higher and the middle guide was moved to ensure that the workpiece is located in the correct position.

normal

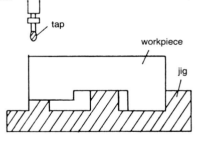

defective

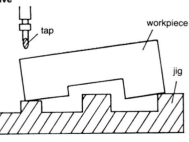

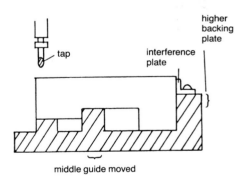

middle guide moved

● *Example 83*

Process: Assembly

Problem: Wrong parts mounted

Solution: Automatic parts bin

Key Improvement: Selection of parts automated

Prevent Error: X

Detect Error:

Shutdown:

Control: X

Alarm:

Description of Process: On an assembly line the model is changed several times a day, and to shorten the time required for model changes, the parts for all the models are stored next to the assembly line.

Before Improvement:

The parts were kept in open boxes and sometimes the operators mounted the wrong parts inadvertently.

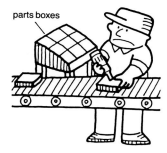

parts boxes

After Improvement:

A rotating parts rack was made, with one delivery outlet. When the selection button is pressed for a particular model, only the parts needed for that model are delivered. It is impossible to take out parts for other models, even accidentally.

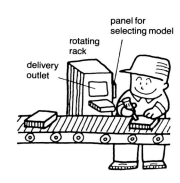

panel for selecting model

rotating rack

delivery outlet

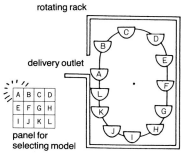

rotating rack

delivery outlet

panel for selecting model

● *Example 84*

Process: Assembling gears

Problem: Two similar gears confused

Solution: Change mounting method and differentiate gears by color

Key Improvement: Part modified to guarantee correct positioning

Prevent Error: X

Detect Error:

Shutdown:

Control: X

Alarm:

Description of Process: A time switch is equipped with a power line frequency selection mechanism so it can be used in areas with either 60 Hz or 50 Hz power sources. The 50 Hz and 60 Hz gears are installed next to each other on the same shaft. There is a difference of only three teeth between these two gears.

Before Improvement:

It was difficult to tell the gears apart with the naked eye, and since they fit interchangeably on the shaft, there were often assembly errors.

After Improvement:

The holes in the gears and the shaft fitting into them were improved as shown in the drawings. In addition, since the gears are made of plastic, the 50 Hz gear is now made of white plastic and the 60 Hz gear is made of blue plastic, so they can be identified at a glance. Installation errors are completely eliminated.

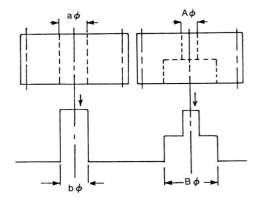

50 Hz gear   60 Hz gear

$a\phi$ $A\phi$

$b\phi$ $B\phi$

$B\phi$ will not fit into $a\phi$

$b\phi$ will not fit into $A\phi$

● *Example 85*

Process: Mounting test jigs

Problem: Test jig mounted backwards

Solution: Interference part on jig

Key Improvement: Jig modified to guarantee correct positioning

Prevent Error: X

Detect Error:

Shutdown:

Control: X

Alarm:

Description of Process: A jig to check the operation of a product is mounted in the process of inspecting the product.

Before Improvement:

It was possible to mount the jig upside down. Even normal products tested abnormally if the jig was mounted upside down. This caused much loss of time. The operators were asked to be careful, but they still tended to mount the jig in the wrong direction accidentally.

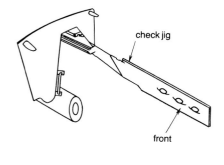

After Improvement:

The jig was remodeled with a raised part on the surface so it is impossible to mount it upside down. The raised part strikes against part A if the operator attempts to mount the jig upside down. This improvement eliminated losses due to mounting errors.

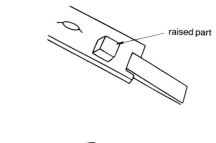

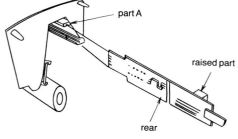

● *Example 86*

Process: Welding

Problem: Workpiece mounted backwards

Solution: Interference block on jig

Key Improvement: Jig modified to guarantee correct positioning

Prevent Error: X

Detect Error:

Shutdown:

Control: X

Alarm:

Description of Process: A workpiece was placed on a jig for a plate to be welded to it.

Before Improvement:

It was possible to unintentionally mount the workpiece on the jig backwards, leading to defects when the plate was welded to the wrong side.

correct

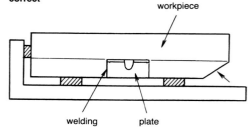

wrong

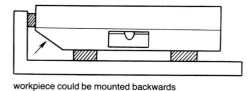

workpiece could be mounted backwards

After Improvement:

A block was installed to prevent the workpiece from being mounted backwards. This eliminates defects.

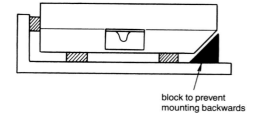

block to prevent mounting backwards

● *Example 87*

Process: Mounting a gear on a shaft

Problem: Gear and shaft aligned incorrectly

Solution: Jig ensures correct alignment

Key Improvement: Jig used to guarantee correct positioning

Prevent Error: X

Detect Error:

Shutdown:

Control: X

Alarm:

Description of Process: A gear is mounted on a shaft and plate assembly inside the transmission case of a rice-planting vehicle. Alignment marks are punched on the shaft assembly and the gear and then must be properly aligned during assembly.

Before Improvement:

On a number of occasions mistakes occurred in aligning the marks. It was necessary to dismantle the units after they had been completed in these cases.

correct

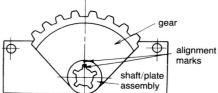

defective

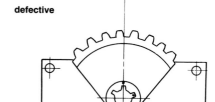

marks not aligned

After Improvement:

A jig was made to ensure that the gear and shaft assembly are properly aligned when assembled. The jig is set over the shaft and positioned using one of the holes in the plate. The long rod on the jig (shown in diagram) then guides the gear along the shaft in the correct orientation.

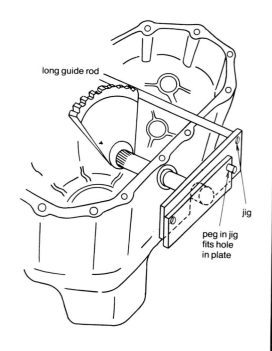

● *Example 88*

Process: Mounting link shaft assemblies

Problem: Mistaking left and right link shaft assemblies

Solution: Improved jig

Key Improvement: Jig used to guarantee correct positioning

Prevent Error: X

Detect Error:

Shutdown:

Control: X

Alarm:

Description of Process: Left and right link shafts with wires attached to them are mounted on a controlling machine.

Before Improvement:

Although the mounting shanks for the left and right link shafts were angled in different directions, the link shafts had a similar appearance in general and were sometimes mounted in reverse, causing defects.

link shaft (right)

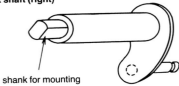

shank for mounting

link shaft (left)

different angle from right shaft

After Improvement:

The link shafts are inserted into separate holding jigs for left and right shafts so that they are accurately sorted before reaching the assembly line.

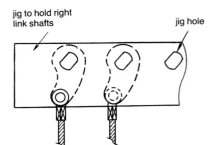

jig to hold right link shafts

jig hole

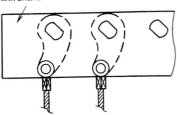

jig to hold left link shafts

left and right marks are etched in the mounting directions of the wires

● *Example 89*

Process: Mounting cleated belts

Problem: Belts mounted backwards

Solution: Improved jig

Key Improvement: Jig modified to guarantee correct positioning

Prevent Error: X

Detect Error:

Shutdown:

Control: X

Alarm:

Description of Process: Cleated belts are mounted on pulleys. If a belt is mounted backwards on the pulley, the teeth on the belt have the wrong orientation.

Before Improvement:

   A plate marked with the proper direction for mounting the cleated belt was placed on the workstand. The operator mounted the belt so the direction of the teeth matched the marks on the plate. However, the belts were sometimes mounted backwards.

plate indicating proper direction to mount cleated belt

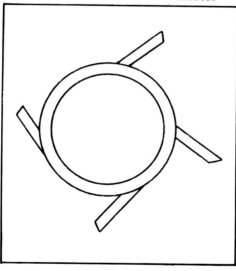

After Improvement:

   The workstand was modified with vertical plates that make it impossible to mount the belts backwards. Defective mounting no longer occurs.

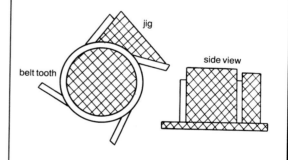

● *Example 90*

Process: Mounting dial pointer	**Prevent Error:** X	**Shutdown:**
Problem: Pointer mounted upside down	**Detect Error:**	**Control:** X
Solution: Improve jig		**Alarm:**

Key Improvement: Jig modified to guarantee correct positioning

Description of Process: A pointer, pointer boss, and washer are mounted to a dial shaft. The pointer is unpainted and it is difficult to tell its front from its back.

Before Improvement:

Although workers were very careful when assembling, they sometimes mistook the back for the front and mounting errors occurred. The defects were discovered after painting at the final assembly stage.

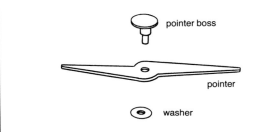

pointer boss

pointer

washer

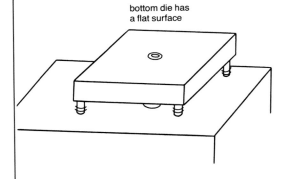

bottom die has a flat surface

After Improvement:

A cutout was made in the bottom die used for mounting the pointer. The cutout makes it impossible to mount the pointer upside down.

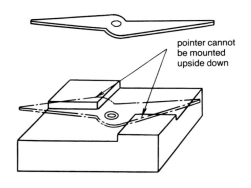

pointer cannot be mounted upside down

● *Example 91*

Process: Series of machining operations

Problem: Similar parts getting confused

Solution: Pin installed on next jig detects omission of processing

Key Improvement: Jig modified to detect defective parts

Prevent Error:

Detect Error: X

Shutdown: X

Control:

Alarm:

Description of Process: Several operations are carried out in series to form a part. For each part, the operations are punching the outside shape, bending twice, punching a notch, and tapping.

Before Improvement:

The notching operation was sometimes skipped. This could not be discovered in the tapping process, and the part would be sent on to assembly where the defect was not discovered until final inspection.

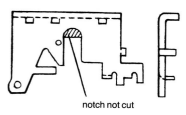

notch not cut

After Improvement:

A pin was added to the tapping jig so the part cannot be mounted for tapping if the notch has not been cut. Parts with uncut notches are now detected early and can be fixed.

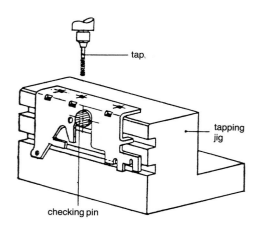

tap

tapping jig

checking pin

● *Example 92*

Process: Assembly line

Problem: Similar parts getting confused

Solution: Automatic parts selection

Key Improvement: Selection of parts automated

Prevent Error: X

Detect Error:

Shutdown:

Control: X

Alarm:

Description of Process: Several different springs are used in the assembly of different models of a switching mechanism. The springs are all similar to one another, and with no identifying marks they are easily confused.

Before Improvement:

The springs were kept on the workbench in a box with open compartments, where they tended to get mixed together and confused. Since correct assembly relied on the operator selecting the correct component, defects occurred.

After Improvement:

The spring storage was modified. A threefold checking method is used, in which checks are made visually, audible signals confirm the checks, and a timer is used for automatic checks. (1) A light is used to indicate which part is in use. (2) The lids on the parts boxes are mounted so that only one type of spring can be used at a time, and the wrong spring cannot be used by mistake. (3) If the lid of a container not in use is not closed within six seconds after the lid of another container is opened, a buzzer sounds, alerting the operator.

Type of spring used

Model \ Name of Part	Main spring	Contact spring	Limit spring
Standard 4-pole			
UL 100A or below			
UL 110A or higher	springs with long A section	springs with long B section	

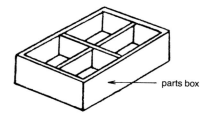

parts box

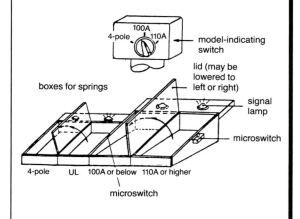

model-indicating switch

lid (may be lowered to left or right)

boxes for springs

signal lamp

microswitch

4-pole UL 100A or below 110A or higher

microswitch

● *Example 93*

Process: Assembly

Problem: Backward mounting

Solution: Modify jig to prevent backward mounting

Key Improvement: Jig modified to guarantee correct positioning

Prevent Error: X

Detect Error:

Shutdown:

Control: X

Alarm:

Description of Process: The main unit is set into an assembly jig, then the cover is set on top and mounted.

Before Improvement:

It was possible to mount the cover in the wrong direction since the positioning block was lower than the height of the cover bracket. This resulted in assembly errors.

After Improvement:

Assembly errors were prevented by raising the height of the positioning blocks on the assembly jig and by adding a bracket-positioning block.

positioning blocks

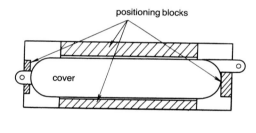

cover

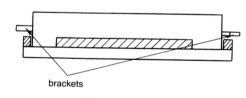

brackets

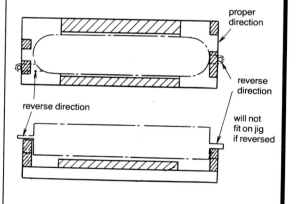

proper direction

reverse direction

reverse direction

will not fit on jig if reversed

● *Example 94*

Process: Installing decorative screws

Problem: Decorative screws were difficult to seat properly

Solution: Change shape of screw

Prevent Error: X

Detect Error:

Shutdown:

Control: X

Alarm:

Key Improvement: Part modified to guarantee correct positioning

Description of Process: Decorative screws are installed on workpieces.

Before Improvement:

The screws were difficult to seat properly. Improperly seated screws could be discovered only during packing, at which time it was necessary to loosen and tighten the screw repeatedly to get it to seat properly. This process became a bottleneck on the assembly line.

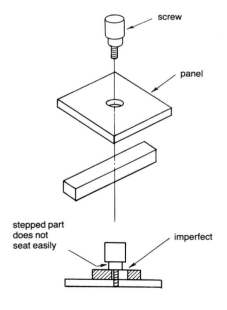

After Improvement:

The shape of the screw was altered. The stepped part on the screw changed to a taper. This makes it possible to tighten the screw right into the hole in one operation.

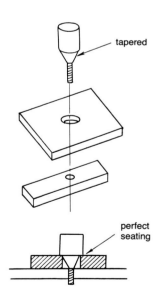

Mounting Errors

● *Example 95*

Process: Mounting small plaques on a panel

Problem: Plaques mounted upside down

Solution: Make mounting pin asymmetrical

Key Improvement: Part modified to guarantee correct positioning

Prevent Error: X

Detect Error:

Shutdown:

Control: X

Alarm:

Description of Process: Small sign plaques are mounted on a panel.

Before Improvement:

Although the workers were careful when mounting the plaques, defects occurred because it was possible to mount them upside down.

After Improvement:

The axis of the mounting pin of the plaque was moved away from the center, making it impossible to mount upside down. Defects due to upside down mounting are completely eliminated. When this improvement is made when fabricating new dies, no extra cost is involved.

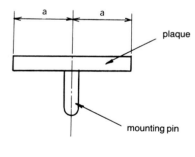

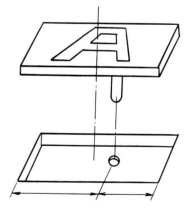

● *Example 96*

Process: Mounting cassette deck control buttons **Prevent Error:** X **Shutdown:**

Problem: Eject buttons mounted upside down **Detect Error:** **Control:** X

Solution: Make mounting pins different diameters **Alarm:**

Key Improvement: Part modified to guarantee correct positioning

Description of Process: Cassette deck eject buttons are mounted onto control arms.

Before Improvement:

Because the eject buttons could be mounted in either direction, they were sometimes mounted upside down.

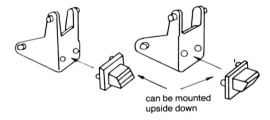

can be mounted upside down

After Improvement:

The diameters of the mounting pins were made unequal. Upside down mounting is impossible, and faulty mounting is completely eliminated.

(1) and (2) have different diameters, so upside down mounting is impossible

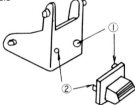

● *Example 97*

Process: Mounting band selector switches in car radios

Problem: Switches mounted upside down

Solution: Make part asymmetrical

Key Improvement: Part modified to guarantee correct positioning

Prevent Error: X

Detect Error:

Shutdown:

Control: X

Alarm:

Description of Process: Band selector switches are mounted in car radio tuners.

Before Improvement:

    The three-band switch circuit board was symmetrical and could be mounted upside down.

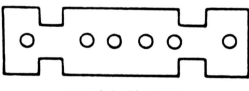

symmetrical on left and right

After Improvement:

    A notch is made on the switch circuit board, as shown in the drawing. The notch corresponds to a raised part on the switch frame to prevent placement errors. Defective mounting of selection switches is completely eliminated.

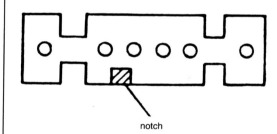

notch

● *Example 98*

Process: Mounting push buttons onto cassette deck control levers

Problem: Buttons mounted upside down

Solution: Make part asymmetrical

Key Improvement: Part modified to guarantee correct positioning

Prevent Error: X

Detect Error:

Shutdown:

Control: X

Alarm:

Description of Process: Push buttons are mounted onto cassette deck control levers.

Before Improvement:

Because the top and bottom shapes were similar, it was difficult to tell the top of a button from the bottom, so push buttons were often mounted upside down.

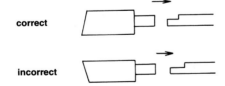

correct

incorrect

After Improvement:

The button and control lever were redesigned using a mortise and tenon joint. It is impossible to mount the push button upside down, so defects no longer occur.

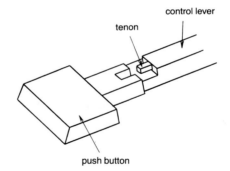

control lever

tenon

push button

● *Example 99*

Process: Mounting battery springs

Problem: Springs mounted to incorrect depth

Solution: Improve mounting tool to measure depth

Key Improvement: Tool modified to test part

Prevent Error: X

Detect Error:

Shutdown:

Control: X

Alarm:

Description of Process: Battery springs are mounted into portable electronic products.

Before Improvement:

An ordinary screwdriver was used to push the springs into the holes, and proper positioning depended on the skill of the workers. However, there were defects because the springs could be pushed down below their proper positions.

ordinary screwdriver

After Improvement:

The tip of the screwdriver was cut as shown so it acts as a stopper or depth gage. Anyone performing the operation now can push the springs to the proper position with no trouble. Defects are completely eliminated.

depth gage

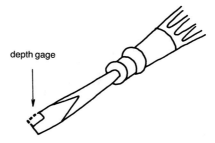

"improved" screwdriver

● *Example 100*

Process: Assembly of TV tuner

Problem: Missing screw holes in TV tuner assembly

Solution: Modify inspection jig to test for screw holes

Key Improvement: Jig modified to detect defective parts

Prevent Error:

Detect Error: X

Shutdown:

Control: X

Alarm:

Description of Process: At one point in the assembly process for TV tuners mounting brackets are added to the chassis for later attachment to the rest of the TV assembly. Sometimes the brackets have not been correctly processed and are missing the required screwholes.

Before Improvement:

Detection of missing screw holes depended on the vigilance of the operators at further processes along the line. However, defects got through to final assembly often and the tuners could not be mounted in the TVs.

After Improvement:

Rods for detecting the presence of the screw holes were mounted on the jig for inspecting the tuner assemblies. The tuner cannot be set in position for quality inspection unless the screw holes are in the proper place. Defective tuners are now detected before being sent on to final assembly.

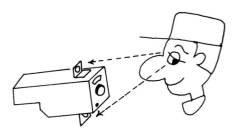

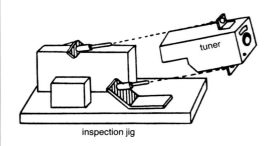

inspection jig

● *Example 101*

Process: Speaker box assembly

Problem: Speaker boxes mounted upside down

Solution: Make part asymmetrical

Key Improvement: Part modified to guarantee correct positioning

Prevent Error: X

Detect Error:

Shutdown:

Control: X

Alarm:

Description of Process: Front plates were attached to speaker boxes.

Before Improvement:

It was difficult to determine the correct orientation of the speaker boxes because the mounting holes were symmetrical at top and bottom. Correct mounting depended exclusively on the workers' vigilance, with the result that the speaker boxes were sometimes mounted to the front plates upside down.

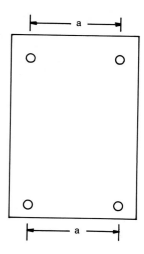

After Improvement:

The positions of the mounting holes were made asymmetrical on the top so that incorrect mounting is impossible. Upside-down mounting is completely eliminated.

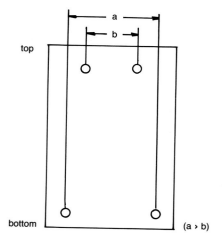

● *Example 102*

Process: Mounting push buttons onto switch levers

Problem: Buttons mounted upside down

Solution: Change parts so they can be mounted only one way

Key Improvement: Part modified to detect guarantee correct positioning

Prevent Error: X

Detect Error:

Shutdown:

Control: X

Alarm:

Description of Process: Push buttons are mounted on switch levers in electronic audio equipment.

Before Improvement:

Push buttons could be inserted upside down as they were mounted.

After Improvement:

Raised and recessed parts are used so the operation will be done correctly even by inexperienced workers. Upside-down mounting is completely eliminated.

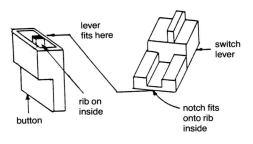

lever fits here

switch lever

rib on inside

button

notch fits onto rib inside

● *Example 103*

Process: Mounting LED frames

Problem: Frames mounted upside down

Solution: Make frame asymmetrical

Key Improvement: Part modified to guarantee correct positioning

Prevent Error: X

Detect Error:

Shutdown:

Control: X

Alarm:

Description of Process: LED output display plates were mounted in a metal frame on an electronic device.

Before Improvement:

   The outside shape of the metal plate was symmetrical, and the plates were sometimes mounted in the frames upside down.

After Improvement:

   Notches were made on one corner of the metal plate and on the matching corner of the frame to ensure that the plate is always mounted correctly. Upside down mounting is completely eliminated.

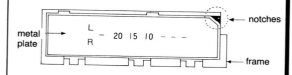

● *Example 104*

Process: Drilling

Problem: 1. Plates drilled upside down
2. Chips on jig, causing misplaced holes

Solution: Improve jig

Key Improvement: Jig modified to guarantee correct positioning

Prevent Error: X

Detect Error:

Shutdown:

Control: X

Alarm:

Description of Process: A multispindle drill press is used to drill holes in covers. The covers are nearly symmetrical on top and bottom, making it difficult for the operator to determine which side is which by visual inspection.

Before Improvement:

1. The covers could be placed in the jig right side up or upside down.
2. Chips from earlier drilling stuck to the covers and interfered with locators on the jig, resulting in misplaced holes.

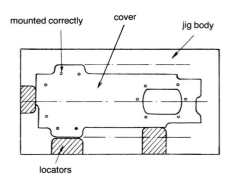

mounted correctly   cover   jig body

locators

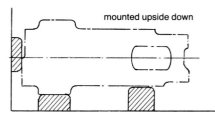

mounted upside down

After Improvement:

The jig was redesigned according to two objectives:
1. Use the slight differences between top and bottom of cover to prevent upside down processing;
2. Reduce contact area of locators on jig so chips won't adhere and interfere with workpiece positioning.

The positions of the locators were changed so covers cannot be mounted upside down. If the workpieces are mounted upside down, they strike against the locators.

The shape of the locators is changed so there is a minimum contacting area, making it difficult for chips to stick there.

These changes make it possible for the operator to mount the workpieces with minimal attention, and processing defects due to mounting errors are completely eliminated.

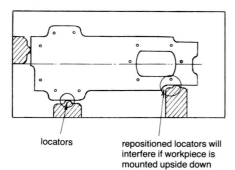

locators   repositioned locators will
                  interfere if workpiece is
                  mounted upside down

● *Example 105*

Process: Spot welding assembly guides to cases

Problem: Assembly guides mounted upside down

Solution: Paint correct side of assembly guide before mounting

Key Improvement: Part modified to show defective processing

Prevent Error:

Detect Error: X

Shutdown:

Control: X

Alarm:

Description of Process: The top and bottom parts of a case, assembled later by the customers, have assembly guides mounted to them by spot welding.

Before Improvement:

Because of the similar shape of the top and bottom parts, it was easy to weld the guides upside down on the cases. However, if the guides were upside down, the cases couldn't be assembled. Some of these defective items were delivered to customers and complaints were received.

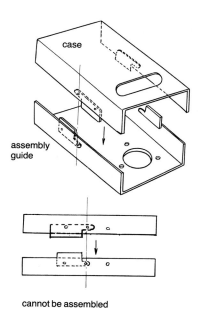

case

assembly guide

cannot be assembled

After Improvement:

The assembly guides are painted red before welding, on the side that faces inside the case. If the red color appears on the outside surface of the guide, the mistake is easily detected.

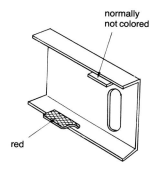

normally not colored

red

● *Example 106*

Process: Mounting back lids

Problem: Back lids mounted upside down

Solution: Limit switch to detect upside down lids

Key Improvement: Procedure added for error detection

Prevent Error:

Detect Error: X

Shutdown:

Control:

Alarm: X

Description of Process: Back lids for housings were mounted in an assembly process.

Before Improvement:

Sometimes the back lids were mistakenly mounted upside down, with the rectangular piece on the wrong end or omitted altogether. The error could not be detected by looking at the external appearance after mounting.

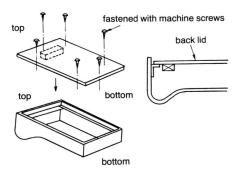

After Improvement:

A system was set up in which an air cylinder pushes one back lid at a time onto a turntable for checking. A motor automatically rotates the turntable, which stops when the rectangular piece hits the limit switch. If the rectangular piece is omitted, the turntable will keep going around, and an alarm buzzer rings after 5 seconds. If the piece is upside down, it trips an alarm switch as it comes out of the hopper. This setup completely eliminated defective assembly of the lids.

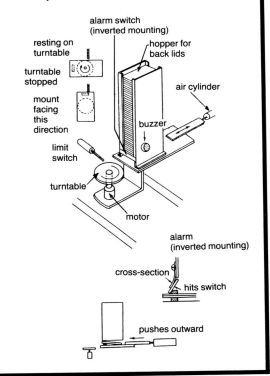

● *Example 107*

Process: Press-fitting shafts to plates

Problem: Shafts reversed end to end

Solution: Use limit switch to detect reversed part

Key Improvement: Operation prevented if part is not positioned

Prevent Error: X

Detect Error:

Shutdown: X

Control:

Alarm: X

Description of Process: A shaft is press-fitted into a metal mounting plate. The shaft is roughly symmetrical end to end.

Before Improvement:

It was possible to set up the shaft backwards for pressing. If a mistake was made when setting up the shaft, a defective item was produced.

incorrect

correct

After Improvement:

A sensor (proximity limit switch) was mounted on the press-fitting machine. The switch is activated when the shaft is set up correctly; a lamp goes on and the press does not operate if the limit switch is not tripped.

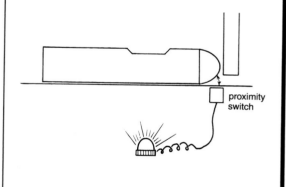

proximity switch

● *Example 108*

Process: Mounting base plates

Problem: Plates mounted upside down

Solution: Mounting jig

Key Improvement: Jig used to guarantee correct positioning

Prevent Error: X

Detect Error:

Shutdown:

Control: X

Alarm:

Description of Process: Base plates were attached to mounting strips to prepare them for further assembly.

Before Improvement:

   Since it was possible to mount the base plates in either direction, correct mounting depended on the workers' vigilance. However, workers inadvertently made errors sometimes and mounted the plates upside down. These defects were not discovered until later assembly.

After Improvement:

   A jig was developed for use in mounting the base plates. The plate is fastened between a guide and a stopper on the jig, making it impossible to mount the plate backwards.

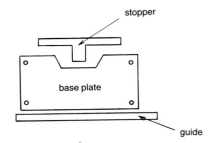

correct

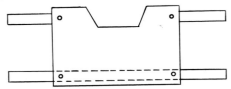

wrong

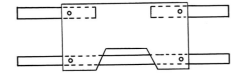

● *Example 109*

Process: Press-fitting parts onto a shaft

Problem: Shafts not set on jig properly

Solution: Coerce part into jig with suction, and detect additional setup errors

Prevent Error: X

Detect Error: X

Shutdown:

Control: X

Alarm: X

Key Improvement: Jig modified to guarantee correct positioning; operation tied to value of critical physical quantity

Description of Process: First a shaft is placed on the jig, then a lever and base plate are set in position and press-fitted onto the shaft.

Before Improvement:

The spot facing on the jig, a depression for the shaft to fit in, was quite shallow (0.3 mm). Therefore, it was easy to place the shaft in the jig at an angle, as shown in the drawing, and when the lever and base plate were press-fitted, a defective unit resulted. The workers did not always notice this defect, and parts with faulty lever movements were sometimes sent on to the next process.

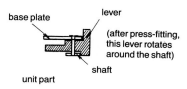

unit part

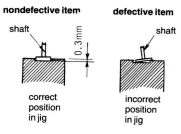

Note: The spot facing on the jig has a shallow depth (.3 mm)

After Improvement:

A small hole was drilled in the center of the jig and a vacuum pump is used to apply suction on the shaft, pulling the shaft down and seating it in the jig. When the lever and base plate are set in position, the shaft does not move. However, since even in this case the shaft might be set at an angle and not seat correctly, an additional improvement has been made. A vacuum gauge is installed in the vacuum line, and if it registers no suction, indicating the shaft is not set correctly, an OFF signal is sent to the press, and the machinery shuts down automatically. This alerts the operator that the shaft is set in place improperly.

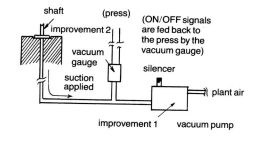

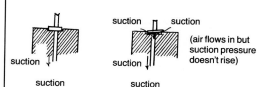

● *Example 110*

Process: Drilling high-precision holes   **Prevent Error:** X   **Shutdown:**

Problem: Chips on jig, causing misaligned holes   **Detect Error:**   **Control:** X

Solution: Microswitch to detect proper placement of part   **Alarm:**

Key Improvement: Operation prevented if part is not positioned

Description of Process: A special drilling machine is used to drill reference position holes for a process in which high-precision small processed parts are assembled. The pin holes are used for positioning references when assembling the parts. It is important that the pin holes be accurately positioned. Since the parts have threads tapped on their inner diameters, the pin holes are positioned by screwing the parts into a reference jig as shown in the drawing. Foreign matter such as chips or shavings adhere to the contacting surface at times, and the positioning can be incorrect as a result.

Before Improvement:

It was not possible to detect small variations in positioning when drilling, so if foreign matter had interfered with the part on the jig, entire lots had to be rejected when the parts arrived at assembly.

After Improvement:

A notch was made on part of the contacting surface of the jig, and a microswitch is mounted there to detect whether the workpiece and the jig are fitting snugly. The switch is connected to a red lamp, which lights when the switch is open, and a blue lamp, which lights when the switch is closed, and to the power switch of the drilling machine. The switch is adjusted so it does not close if there are chips on the jig, so drilling cannot begin unless there is nothing caught on the jig. Setting errors have been completely eliminated.

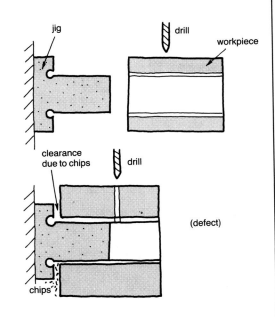

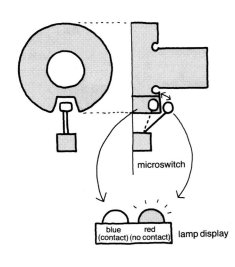

● *Example 111*

Process: Circuit board assembly

Problem: Parts mounted in wrong position

Solution: Build gage into assembly jig

Key Improvement: Jig modified to guarantee correct positioning

Prevent Error: X

Detect Error:

Shutdown:

Control: X

Alarm:

Description of Process: Various electronic parts are inserted and soldered onto circuit boards. The design of the enclosure requires that the parts extend 10 mm or less from the edges of the circuit board.

Before Improvement:

After mounting the parts, the workers used a gage to check that the parts were within 10 mm of the edge of the board. However, these checks were sometimes omitted, allowing defective circuit boards to be passed along to the next process.

After Improvement:

The gage was incorporated into the mounting jig so that it is impossible for the part to extend 10 mm or further after assembly. The process is now always performed correctly even without the workers' conscious awareness that they are testing.

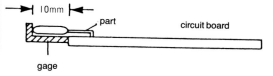

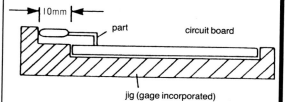

● *Example 112*

Process: Mounting automobile wire harness guides   **Prevent Error:** X   **Shutdown:**

Problem: Wire guides mounted upside down   **Detect Error:**   **Control:** X

Solution: Improve mounting jig   **Alarm:**

Key Improvement: Jig modified to guarantee correct positioning

Description of Process: Brackets for wire harnesses are mounted on the floors of automobiles.

Before Improvement:

The jig permitted the wire guides to be mounted upside down by mistake.

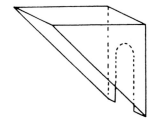

correct position

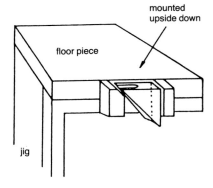

floor piece

mounted upside down

jig

After Improvement:

The jig was improved so that a pin catches on the hole in the wire guide through which the wire harnesses pass. The guide can be mounted only in the correct orientation, thus eliminating mounting defects.

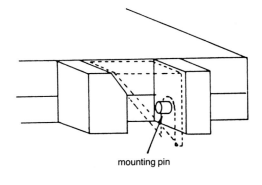

mounting pin

● *Example 113*

Process: Drilling

Problem: Holes drilled in wrong positions

Solution: Improve jig

Key Improvement: Jig modified to guarantee correct positioning

Prevent Error: X

Detect Error:

Shutdown:

Control: X

Alarm:

Description of Process: Plates are drilled on a multispindle drill press.

Before Improvement:

The jig used for setting up the workpieces allowed the workpiece to be drilled upside down or rotated. Defects were frequently turned out when the holes were drilled with the plates set up incorrectly. These defects were not usually found until the assembly process, and clients were inconvenienced by delays in delivery.

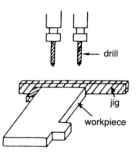

correctly drilled

defective items

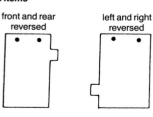

After Improvement:

The jig was improved to eliminate drilling defects. The additional guides on the jig prevent the plates from being mounted incorrectly.

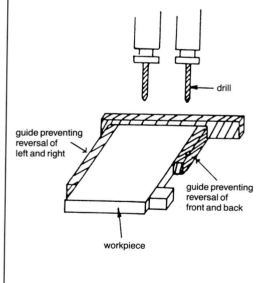

● Example 114

Process: Welding plates

Problem: Plates welded upside down

Solution: Improve jig to prevent setting up plate upside down

Key Improvement: Jig modified to guarantee correct positioning

Prevent Error: X

Detect Error:

Shutdown:

Control: X

Alarm:

Description of Process: Plates are set in a jig to be welded. The plates have protrusions on the side that is supposed to be up.

Before Improvement:

The jig did not prevent the worker from setting up the plate upside down, so the worker was supposed to check that the protrusions were up before welding. However, workers sometimes welded on the wrong surface, although they thought they were being careful.

correct position

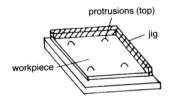

incorrect position

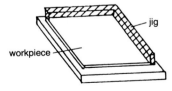

After Improvement:

The jig was remodeled so it is impossible for the worker to set the workpiece in position upside down. The new jig has an additional guide with notches for the protrusions on the top surface. If the plate is mounted upside down, the new guide prevents the plate from being set against the other guides. Welding on the wrong surface of the plates has been completely eliminated.

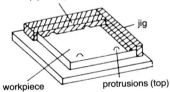

correct

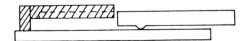

cannot be set in position

● *Example 115*

Process: Mounting brushes on vacuum cleaner attachments

Problem: Missing brushes

Solution: Detect missing brushes during automatic assembly and during delivery to next process

Key Improvement: Tool modified to guarantee correct processing; chute modified to sort out defective parts

Prevent Error: X

Detect Error: X

Alarm:

Shutdown: X

Control: X

Description of Process: Two brushes are mounted by an automatic machine onto a vacuum cleaner head attachment.

Before Improvement:

Sometimes the brushes were not mounted, due to errors in the machinery. An inspector was specially assigned to check each vacuum attachment to determine whether both brushes had been mounted.

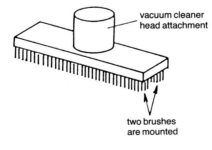

vacuum cleaner head attachment

two brushes are mounted

After Improvement:

Two improvements were made to ensure that both brushes are mounted:

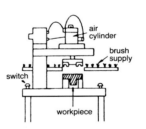

air cylinder

brush supply

switch

workpiece

1. Several sensors were added to the assembly machine to detect when the brush supply is empty. The machine does not operate if there are no brushes to mount, and an alarm sounds automatically.

chute

block

2. A delivery chute was provided for putting the finished vacuum attachments into boxes for delivery. A block is mounted in the chute and does not let defective attachments pass. If one of the brushes is missing, the block prevents the defective unit from passing through.

nondefective item

block

defective item

● *Example 116*

Process: Mounting drawer rails on cabinet sides

Problem: Drawer rails mounted in wrong positions

Solution: Improved jig

Key Improvement: Jig modified to guarantee correct positioning

Prevent Error: X

Detect Error:

Shutdown:

Control: X

Alarm:

Description of Process: Drawer rails are mounted on cabinet sides using one jig for both left and right sides.

Before Improvement:

Mounting errors had been quite noticeable. In some cases errors were caused by the mounting jig slipping. In other cases, the operator forgot to reverse the mounting jig when changing between left and right cabinet sides. Misalignment of the drawer rails resulted in faulty operation of the drawers or made it impossible to mount the drawers at all.

After Improvement:

The drawer rail mounting jig was set into a workbench so it cannot slip. The mounting method also ensures that the jig is correctly positioned for mounting rails on either the left or right cabinet sides. Errors in mounting the drawer rails no longer occur.

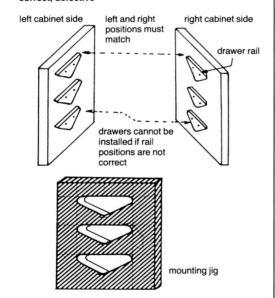

correct, defective

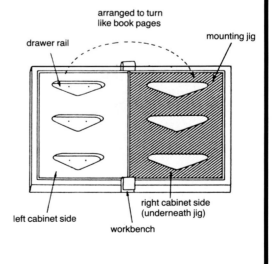

● *Example 117*

Process: Mounting covers

Problem: Left and right covers interchanged

Solution: Improve jig

Key Improvement: Jig modified to guarantee correct positioning

Prevent Error: X

Detect Error:

Shutdown:

Control: X

Alarm:

Description of Process: Left and right covers are mounted at the same time on the same jig. The covers are exactly symmetrical left to right, centering around A, with the exception of the long hole at position 2.

Before Improvement:

It was possible to set the right and left covers in either position on the jig, and sometimes they were mounted in reverse inadvertently.

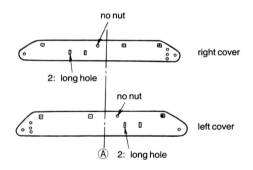

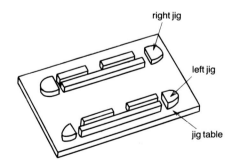

After Improvement:

Target pins were mounted on the jig so it is impossible to mount the covers in reverse. Processing defects due to incorrect mounting are eliminated completely.

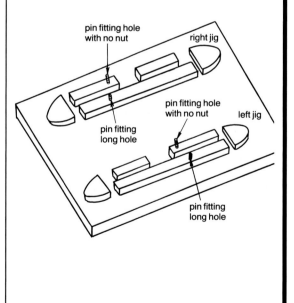

● *Example 118*

Process: Welding shafts to plates	**Prevent Error:** X	**Shutdown:**
Problem: Shafts mounted with ends reversed	**Detect Error:**	**Control:** X
Solution: Improve jig		**Alarm:**

Key Improvement: Jig modified to guarantee correct positioning

Description of Process: Shafts are set in a jig and welded to a plate. The only difference in shape between the ends of the shafts is that a C-ring groove is cut in the end that should not be welded.

Before Improvement:

The jig allowed the shafts to be set up backwards with the groove on the welding end. The workers made visual inspections of the shafts when they were set up, but sometimes the shafts were accidentally welded to the plates backwards. The faulty welding was discovered only at the assembly stage.

After Improvement:

A guide that fits into the groove for the C-ring was mounted on the jig. The guide makes it impossible to set the shaft in position backwards.

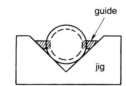

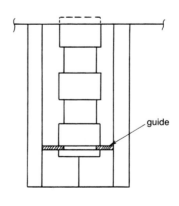

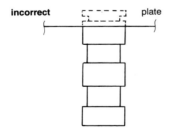

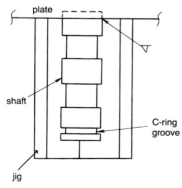

● *Example 119*

Process: Spot welding angle iron

Problem: Welding performed on wrong surface

Solution: Improve jig

Key Improvement: Jig modified to guarantee correct positioning

Prevent Error: X

Detect Error:

Shutdown:

Control: X

Alarm:

Description of Process: An angle iron is set up on a jig and welded. One side of the angle iron has a trough formed in it, making it "wider" than the other side when viewed edge-on. It is important for the trough side to be on the top of the jig, which is notched to hold the trough.

Before Improvement:

A plate spring was used to clamp the angle iron in place for welding. The spring permitted the trough side of the angle iron to be set on the side of the jig instead of the top, resulting in defective welding.

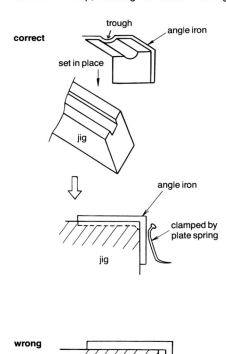

After Improvement:

The jig was improved with a fixed guide to hold the angle iron. The trough side of the angle iron does not fit inside this guide to seat in the jig, so it is impossible to weld to the wrong surface.

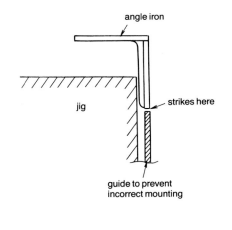

● *Example 120*

Process: Assembly of control levers

Problem: Levers mounted backwards

Solution: Improve assembly jig

Key Improvement: Jig modified to guarantee correct positioning

Prevent Error: X

Detect Error:

Shutdown:

Control: X

Alarm:

Description of Process: Control levers are mounted on the workpiece.

Before Improvement:

Although the correct direction for mounting the control levers was inked with a felt-tip marker on the assembly jig, levers were still sometimes mounted facing the wrong way.

After Improvement:

A block was installed on the assembly jig to prevent the levers from being mounted the wrong way. It is now impossible to mount the levers incorrectly.

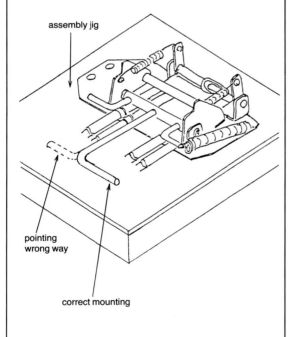

assembly jig

pointing wrong way

correct mounting

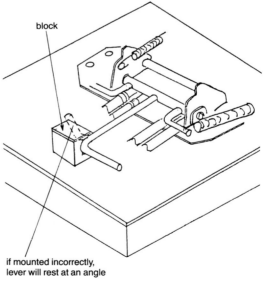

block

if mounted incorrectly, lever will rest at an angle

● *Example 121*

Process: Machining

Problem: Part mounted backwards

Solution: Install interference pin in jig

Key Improvement: Jig modified to guarantee correct positioning

Prevent Error: X

Detect Error:

Shutdown:

Control: X

Alarm:

Description of Process: A certain part is mounted in a jig on a milling machine, then a swing cutter is used to machine the part.

Before Improvement:

It was possible to mount the part in the jig with its left and right sides reversed. The mounting position was checked visually by the worker, but the parts were still sometimes mounted backwards. When the part was mounted backwards the blade machined the part in the wrong place, causing defects.

After Improvement:

A bolt was installed on the mounting table, in a position corresponding to the position of the through hole in the part. It is impossible to mount the part backwards because the bolt prevents the part from seating properly when in the incorrect position.

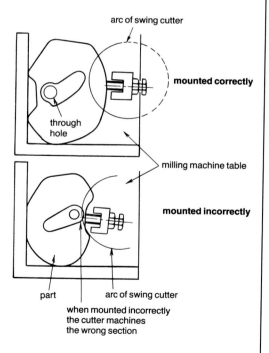

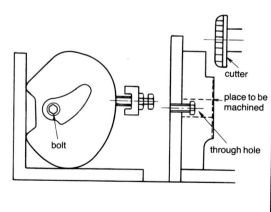

● *Example 122*

Process: Assembly line

Problem: Incorrect parts used

Solution: Automatic parts box

Key Improvement: Selection of parts automated

Prevent Error: X

Detect Error:

Shutdown:

Control: X

Alarm:

Description of Process: Different models are manufactured on the same assembly line, and various similar parts are used on the different models.

Before Improvement:

The parts belonging to different models were color-coded and the operator selected and mounted parts according to the colors. However, errors still occurred fairly easily.

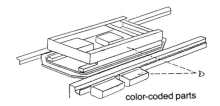

visually determine model

color-coded parts

After Improvement:

A completely mistake-proof solution was devised on the process side, rather than the parts side.

1. Photoelectric switches detect which model is being assembled. A light comes on indicating the proper part. The operator watches for the light and selects the parts to mount accordingly.

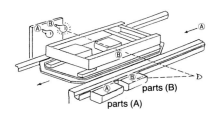

parts (B)

parts (A)

2. The lids on the part boxes slide open and closed automatically, allowing the operator to select only the correct parts for the given model.

These improvements make it unnecessary for the operator to make any judgments, and the operator can now concentrate on operations and on reducing the number of assembly defects.

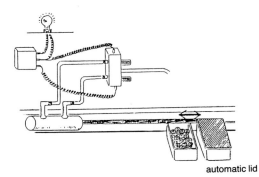

automatic lid

● *Example 123*

Process: Mounting guide rails on car radio sets

Problem: Omission or incorrect mounting of guide rails

Solution: Jig

Key Improvement: Jig modified to detect defective parts

Prevent Error:

Detect Error: X

Shutdown:

Control: X

Alarm:

Description of Process: Guide rails for mounting to car bodies are mounted to car radio sets for insertion into dashboards.

Before Improvement:

Visual checks were made to see that the rails were mounted. However, missing and incorrectly mounted rails were often discovered later.

After Improvement:

A jig with guide-rails cradles is now used for adjustment operations on the radio sets. If the guide rails are missing or not mounted correctly, the set will not be stable in the jig and the defective mounting is discovered. This safeguard completely eliminates missing or incorrectly mounted guide rails.

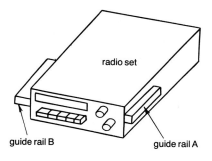

radio set

guide rail B

guide rail A

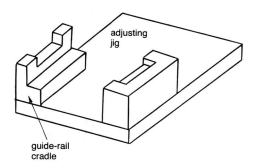

adjusting jig

guide-rail cradle

● *Example 124*

Process: Milling	**Prevent Error:** X	**Shutdown:** X
Problem: Workpieces fly off if they are not fastened down	**Detect Error:**	**Control:**
Solution: Detect when pieces are not fastened down		**Alarm:**

Key Improvement: Tool modified to protect operator from danger

Description of Process: Workpieces to be milled are set onto a spindle and fastened by inserting a U-shaped washer and turning a nut. The workpieces are then processed by the milling machine.

Before Improvement:

It was possible to operate the milling machine even if the U-shaped washer was not inserted to clamp down the workpiece. For quick changeover, the nut was smaller than the core of the workpiece and this resulted in a dangerous situation because the workpiece could fly off the spindle during processing.

After Improvement:

If the workpiece is not clamped with the U-shaped washer, the nut and spindle drop down far below the normal operating position. A limit switch, interlocked with the milling machine power switch, was installed below the spindle to detect this condition. The milling machine can no longer be turned on if the U-shaped washer is not installed.

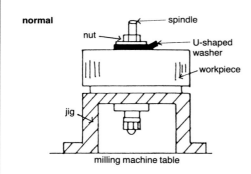

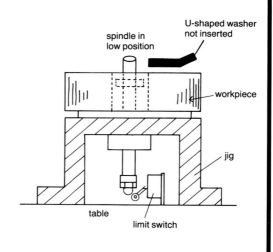

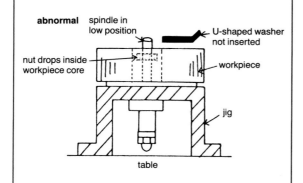

● *Example 125*

Process: Bonding information plate to timer lid

Problem: Plates not mounted or not bonded strongly enough

Solution: Change process from bonding with adhesive to molding information plate into timer lid

Key Improvement: Procedure modified to guarantee correct processing

Prevent Error: X

Detect Error:

Shutdown:

Control: X

Alarm:

Description of Process: An information plate must be attached to the lid of the timer assembly.

Before Improvement:

The information plate was bonded to the timer lid with an adhesive. However, there were variations in the bonding strength, and sometimes the plates were not mounted at all.

After Improvement:

The bonding process itself has so many deficiencies that it is more efficient to use a different process for mounting the information plate and mount the plate integrally from the beginning. Now the information plate is inserted in a die and molded into the timer lid. These integral plates cannot peel off and mounting is never omitted.

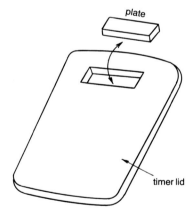

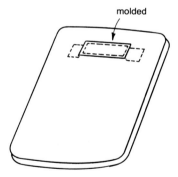

● Example 126

Process: Automated screw-mounting

Problem: Omitted screws not discovered until final assembly

Solution: Detect omission of screws

Key Improvement: Tool modified to detect defective parts

Prevent Error:

Detect Error: X

Shutdown:

Control:

Alarm: X

Description of Process: Brackets are screw-mounted with an automatic screw-mounting machine.

Before Improvement:

Occasionally the screws got stuck in the machine or the operator forgot to supply screws to the machine. As result, parts lacking screws would be passed down the line. The missing screws were usually discovered in the final assembly process. However, in several cases defective products were delivered to the clients, which was a serious problem.

After Improvement:

A detecting device was installed directly after the screw-mounting process. One part of the detector senses the bracket part and another part detects the presence of the screws. If the detector does not sense two screws within five seconds after a bracket is detected, an alarm buzzer sounds to alert the operator.

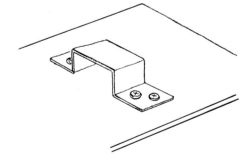

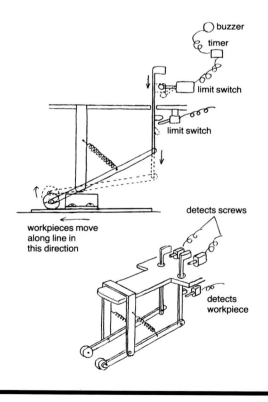

● *Example 127*

Process: Spot welding washers to workpiece

Problem: Omission of washers not discovered until final installation

Solution: Detect omission in subsequent process

Key Improvement: Jig modified to detect defective parts

Prevent Error:

Detect Error: X

Shutdown:

Control:

Alarm: X

Description of Process: Plate washers for mounting installation screws are spot welded to the inside of an iron channel. It is nearly impossible to inspect the washers from the outside.

Before Improvement:

When the welding operation was omitted, it was quite difficult to discover the omission by inspection. However, the omission made it impossible to install the product and led to extensive damages.

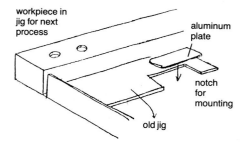

After Improvement:

A jig used in a subsequent process (pasting on an aluminum plate) was remodeled to detect the presence of the washer. The remodeled jig uses the difference in size between the external hole and the washer screw hole. A pin that will pass through the screw hole but not the hole in the washer is installed on the jig. If the pin falls all the way through, the operator can tell that the washer has been omitted.

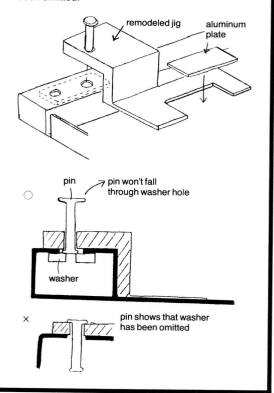

Inclusion of Wrong Items

● *Example 128*

Process: Magnetizing flywheels

Problem: Process omitted

Solution: Detect magnetization using proximity switch

Key Improvement: Procedure added for error detection

Prevent Error:

Detect Error: X

Shutdown:

Control:

Alarm: X

Description of Process: Flywheels are individually magnetized by being passed through a magnetizing machine.

Before Improvement:

The worker placed a flywheel in the magnetizing machine, magnetized the flywheel, then placed it on a table for temporary storage. After the worker processed twenty pieces, the flywheels were checked with a screwdriver to make sure each was magnetized. Sometimes the worker inadvertently skipped the magnetizing process and did not detect the unmagnetized flywheels with the screwdriver test.

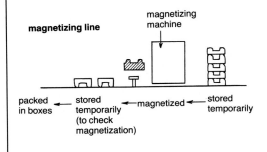

magnetizing line

magnetizing machine

packed in boxes ← stored temporarily (to check magnetization) ← magnetized ← stored temporarily

checking magnetization with a screwdriver

check one of the four poles

After Improvement:

The temporary storage on the table and the screwdriver test were replaced by a conveyor belt and a proximity switch to detect magnetization. The items are passed one by one under the detector and a warning lamp lights if an unmagnetized flywheel is detected, alerting the operator.

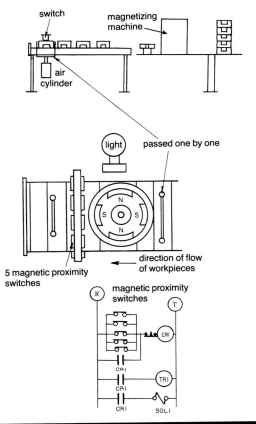

switch

magnetizing machine

air cylinder

light

passed one by one

direction of flow of workpieces

5 magnetic proximity switches

magnetic proximity switches

● *Example 129*

Process: Low-volume production of a variety of products

Problem: Parts for different products mixing together

Solution: Tidying up between products

Key Improvement: Procedure added for error detection

Prevent Error: X

Detect Error:

Shutdown:

Control: X

Alarm:

Description of Process: Low volumes of a variety of products (soft steel, alloy steel, etc.) are produced in a process that used to produce a high volume of a single product.

Before Improvement:

Serious problems developed when parts from one product were mixed with parts of another type after a product changeover.

After Improvement:

A tidying-up step was added to the standard procedure for changing production runs. The worker checks the processing machines for unprocessed parts, and checks the corners and nooks and crannies of the washing cage and transport box for leftover items. This step adds fifteen minutes to the six-hour processing time, but the problems are completely eliminated.

conveyor A

conveyor B

processing machine A

processing machine B

processing machine C

box for finished items

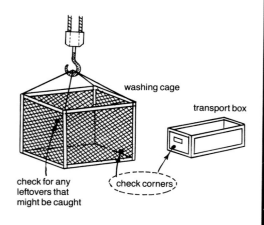

washing cage

transport box

check for any leftovers that might be caught

check corners

● Example 130

Process: Assembly line

Problem: Similar parts confused

Solution: Mechanical system to sort parts

Key Improvement: Chute modified to sort out defective parts

Prevent Error: X

Detect Error:

Shutdown:

Control: X

Alarm:

Description of Process: Many distinct but similar parts are used at a certain station on an assembly line.

Before Improvement:

Items such as those shown caused great difficulty because (1) the parts were very much alike and (2) the two ends of individual parts were very similar.

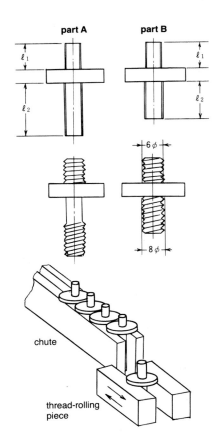

After Improvement:

Several mechanical systems were designed to ensure that incorrect parts are detected before they cause problems. In the example shown, the up-thrust plate detects parts put into the chute upside down, by raising the parts that are right side up. Additional systems (not shown) remove the detected parts.

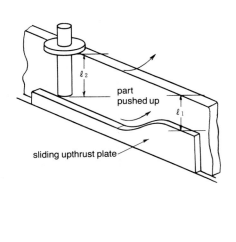

● *Example 131*

Process: Various

Problem: Unidentifiable leftover materials

Solution: Improved color coding

Key Improvement: Procedure modified to guarantee correct processing

Prevent Error: X

Detect Error:

Shutdown:

Control: X

Alarm:

Description of Process: Various processes use different types of metal stock and wire.

Before Improvement:

Different types of metal stock and wire (alloy steel, soft steel, etc.) were identified by colored marks painted on before use. However, many leftover materials were not identifiable after processing because the colored marks had been cut off and the new ends were not repainted. As a result, the wrong materials were sometimes used in processing.

After Improvement:

Instead of having to repaint identifying colors after the material is used, material is painted directly in several places after it has been received and inspected. Identifying colors are placed on both ends of bar stock, and at both ends and two places around the circumference of wire coils. This eliminates unidentifiable leftovers and ensures that products are not manufactured with the wrong materials.

round bar

hexagonal or square bar

wire

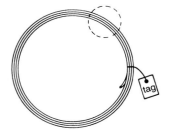

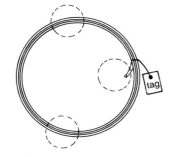

● *Example 132*

Process: Automated parts feeder on assembly line   **Prevent Error:**   **Shutdown:**

Problem: Unprocessed parts delivered to final assembly   **Detect Error:**   X   **Control:**   X

Solution: Mechanical system to detect unprocessed parts   **Alarm:**

Key Improvement: Chute modified to sort out defective parts

Description of Process: An automated parts feeder supplies lever pins to an automatic assembly process.

Before Improvement:

A chute fed lever pins to the automated assembly process. However, some of the lever pins were not completely processed, and the area below the head of the pin was not cut away. These unprocessed pins were assembled along with the good ones. To detect the 0.03 percent units per day assembled with unprocessed pins, workers had to manually inspect and sort the entire output.

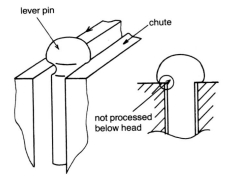

After Improvement:

The feed chute was modified so that only properly processed lever pins can be used for assembly. Because the incompletely processed lever pins do not fit down the delivery chute, a sensor and pneumatic ejection device can detect and remove defective pins from the supply line. This completely eliminates assembly defects.

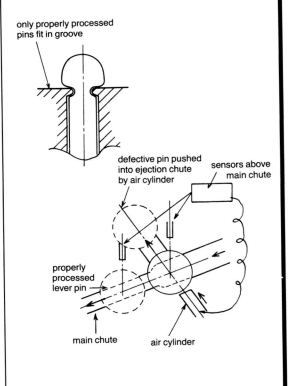

● *Example 133*

Process: Camera lens assembly

Problem: Incorrect lenses assembled into final product

Solution: Better measurement before assembly

Key Improvement: Tool modified to detect defective parts

Prevent Error:

Detect Error: X

Shutdown:

Control:

Alarm: X

Description of Process: Many different lenses are used in this process, all similar in diameter, thickness, and curvature. The differences are impossible to detect with the naked eye.

Before Improvement:

The lenses supplied to the assembly line at any given time were supposed to be correct for the final assembly. However, lenses with the wrong dimensions were occasionally supplied and the error could not be detected until final inspection. The defective assemblies had to be completely disassembled and repaired, at large expense.

After Improvement:

A small electrical micrometer was mounted on the assembly tool. It detects differences in the thickness and curvature of the lenses. If a lens is outside certain limits, an alarm buzzer sounds.

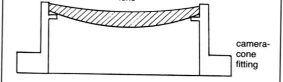

lens

camera-
cone
fitting

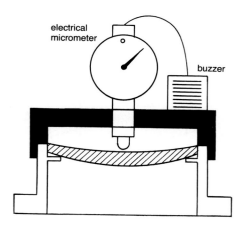

electrical
micrometer

buzzer

● *Example 134*

Process: Camera film plate assembly

Problem: Similar parts confused during assembly

Solution: Photoelectric detector to differentiate parts

Key Improvement: Jig modified to detect defective parts

Prevent Error: X

Detect Error:

Shutdown: X

Control:

Alarm:

Description of Process: Film plates for general use are riveted to one type of film plate spring, and film plates with a dating function cutout are riveted to another type of film plate spring. A rotating table is used that allows six parts to be riveted at the same time.

Before Improvement:

Sometimes the wrong parts were included because of leftovers from the previous run or mix-ups during setup. If the worker failed to notice the problem, the incorrect parts were riveted and defective assemblies were sent to the next process.

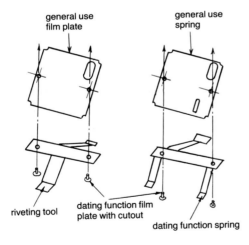

After Improvement:

A light source and photoelectric sensor were mounted on the assembly jig. The sensor detects the presence or absence of the dating function cutout in the film plate. If film plates for general use are being assembled on general-use springs, and the sensor detects a film plate with a dating function cutout, the table is stopped, a buzzer sounds, and riveting cannot proceed. Similarly, the sensor will detect a film plate without a dating function cutout if dating function film plates are being assembled on dating function springs. Processing is stopped before defects are produced; film plate assembly defects have been completely eliminated.

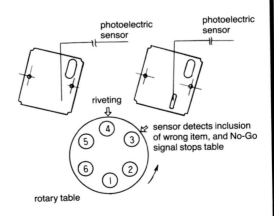

● *Example 135*

Process: Part feed for assembly process

Problem: Similar parts confused

Solution: Mechanical sorting

Key Improvement: Chute modified to sort out defective parts

Prevent Error: X

Detect Error:

Shutdown:

Control: X

Alarm:

Description of Process: Shafts are put into a chute and fed into an assembly process.

Before Improvement:

Operators sometimes accidentally used long shafts made for another process, which caused stoppages and delays in the assembly process.

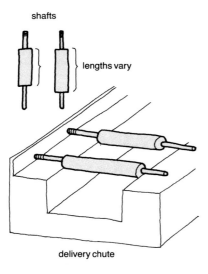

shafts

lengths vary

delivery chute

After Improvement:

An adjustable gage was installed on the chute to ensure that only the proper size of shaft passes down the chute to assembly. If a shaft is too long, the gage blocks the chute and the wrong piece can be removed.

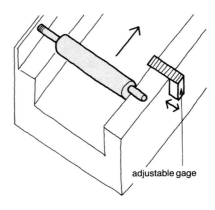

adjustable gage

● *Example 136*

Process: Output from spot welding process   **Prevent Error:**   **Shutdown:**

Problem: Parts with nuts spot welded to the wrong side   **Detect Error:**   X   **Control:**   X

Solution: Mechanical detector   **Alarm:**

Key Improvement: Chute modified to sort out defective parts

Description of Process: The output of a spot welding process in which nuts are welded to small plates is directed along a chute to the delivery box. Some of the parts are incorrectly processed and have the nut welded to the wrong side of the plate.

Before Improvement:

   The defective parts were not detected and were delivered along with the good parts to the next process.

After Improvement:

   A small interference bar was added to the chute to detect defective parts. If a part has the nut welded on the wrong side of the plate, it gets stuck in the chute, where it can be removed and prevented from being delivered to the next process.

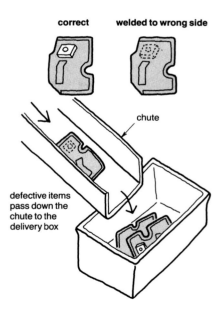

correct   welded to wrong side

chute

defective items pass down the chute to the delivery box

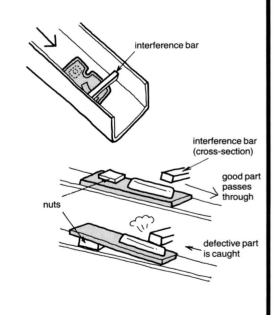

interference bar

interference bar (cross-section)

good part passes through

nuts

defective part is caught

● *Example 137*

Process: Press-fitting

Problem: Similar parts were confused

Solution: Modify one part, modify jigs

Key Improvement: Part and jig modified to guarantee correct positioning

Prevent Error: X

Detect Error:

Shutdown:

Control: X

Alarm:

Description of Process: A number of small pins are press-fitted into two plates (A and B) that are similar. The only difference between A and B is the diameter of one hole, which is 3.0 mm in A and 2.7 mm in B.

Before Improvement:

The jig used when press-fitting the pins into plates A and B did not differentiate between the two parts. As a result, the two plates were often confused during assembly, causing defects.

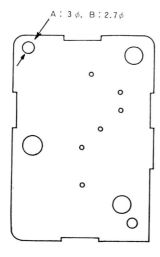

After Improvement:

An additional hole was drilled in plate B and new jigs were developed. Part A does not fit on the jig for part B because of the guide for the extra hole in part B. Likewise, a 3.0 mm pin guide on the jig for part A keeps part B from fitting on the jig.

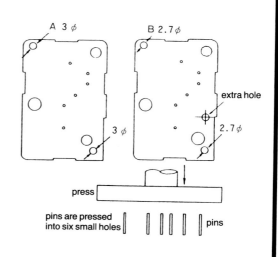

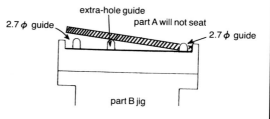

● *Example 138*

Process:	Deburring molded parts	**Prevent Error:**	**Shutdown:**
Problem:	Similar parts manufactured in same step not sorted correctly	**Detect Error:** X	**Control:**
Solution:	Use photoelectric detector to sort		**Alarm:** X

Key Improvement: Tool modified to detect defective parts

Description of Process: Two similar parts are molded with a single die, then sorted and separated by hand during deburring.

Before Improvement:

Because of inadvertent mistakes while sorting, the two parts were sometimes mixed together. Customers complained when they received mixed up parts in their deliveries.

parts molded together

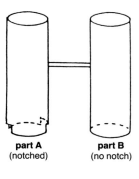

part A
(notched)   **part B**
(no notch)

After Improvement:

A photoelectric detector was installed on the jig used in the deburring process. The parts are rotated, and if any light is detected, it is part A. If no light is detected, it is part B. The operator sorts the parts correctly with this device.

part A

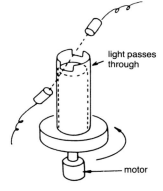

light passes through

motor

part B

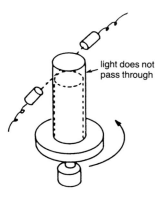

light does not pass through

● *Example 139*

Process: Testing integrated circuits (ICs)

Problem: Defective ICs placed in "good" box after testing

Solution: Electromechanical sorting based on results of testing

Key Improvement: Chute modified to sort out defective parts

Prevent Error:

Detect Error: X

Alarm:

Shutdown:

Control: X

Description of Process: An IC tester is used to measure the characteristic values of ICs against reference values. Those matching the reference values are put into a "good" box, while those deviating from the reference values are placed in a "defective" box.

Before Improvement:

Because of operators' errors, some of the defective ICs were placed in the box with the ICs that tested good. When these ICs were used by customers, the company received complaints.

After Improvement:

A sorting device was developed as shown in the drawing. The gate to the "defective" and "good" boxes moves according to whether the IC has tested good or defective. The operator merely places the IC in the chute after testing and the chute itself decides which box to put the IC in. Mix-ups between defective and good items are eliminated.

inspection

good items

defective items

"good" box

"defective" box

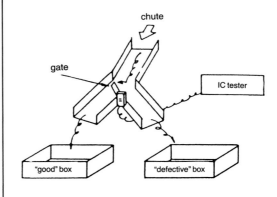

chute

gate

IC tester

"good" box

"defective" box

● *Example 140*

Process: Assembly line

Problem: Wrong parts on line

Solution: Limit switch detector

Key Improvement: Tool modified to detect defective parts

Prevent Error:

Detect Error: X

Shutdown:

Control:

Alarm: X

Description of Process: On an assembly line with many model changes, workers sometimes keep parts along the line that don't belong to the current model. Occasionally the wrong parts are used on the line and sent on to the mounting process. The only difference between the two parts is a raised step on one part that is not on the other.

Before Improvement:

Operators made visual checks to determine if the raised step was present, but sometimes the check was omitted or was mistaken, and the wrong parts moved along the line to the mounting process, where they caused trouble during mounting.

correct part

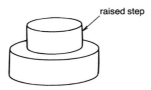

raised step

wrong part

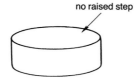

no raised step

After Improvement:

A guide plate and a limit switch were provided on the line conveyor so the wrong parts can be detected automatically. This reduces the number of items to be checked visually and speeds up the line.

correct part

switch is turned on

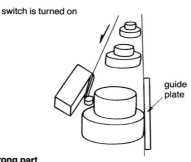

guide plate

wrong part

switch is not turned on

↓

conveyor stops

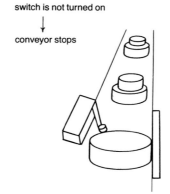

Insertion Errors

● *Example 141*

Process: Mounting electrical shield cases

Problem: Cases mounted backward causing short circuit

Solution: Make shield cases asymmetrical

Prevent Error: X

Detect Error:

Shutdown:

Control: X

Alarm:

Key Improvement: Part modified to guarantee correct positioning

---

Description of Process: A metal shield case is mounted on a printed circuit board. The case has a cutout on one side intended to avoid a trace on the circuit board.

Before Improvement:

The mounting tabs on the case were the same size, so the case could be mounted backwards. Worker vigilance was relied on for mounting the cases correctly. When a case was mounted backwards, it contacted the trace on the circuit board, causing a defective circuit.

After Improvement:

The mounting tabs on the case and the matching slots in the circuit board were made different sizes so the case can be mounted only the right way. Defective mounting is eliminated.

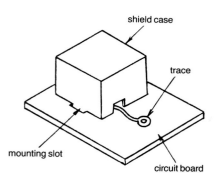

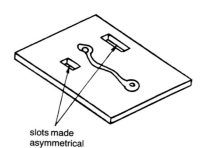

slots made asymmetrical

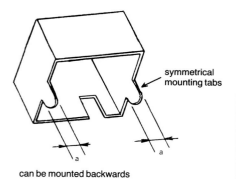

can be mounted backwards

● *Example 142*

Process: Mounting LEDs for cassette deck level meters   **Prevent Error:**   X   **Shutdown:**

Problem: LEDs mounted with wrong polarity   **Detect Error:**   **Control:**   X

Solution: Improved LED holder   **Alarm:**

Key Improvement: Part modified to guarantee correct positioning

Description of Process: Light emitting diodes (LEDs) are soldered onto circuit boards to make cassette deck VU or level meters.

Before Improvement:

It was possible to insert LEDs into the holders backwards, resulting in polarity defects.

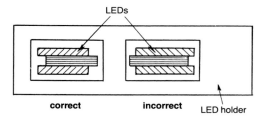

LEDs

correct   **incorrect**   LED holder

can be inserted in either direction

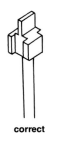   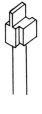

correct   **incorrect**

After Improvement:

An extremely effective improvement was made based on the differences in shapes of the LED and the holder. The holder is changed so that if the operator attempts to insert the LED backwards, a part of the holder interferes with a part of the LED case and LEDs cannot be inserted. Mounting (polarity) errors are completely eliminated.

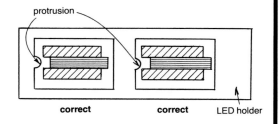

protrusion

correct   **correct**   LED holder

● *Example 143*

Process: Circuit board assembly   **Prevent Error:** X   **Shutdown:**

Problem: Plugs inserted into extra holes   **Detect Error:**   **Control:** X

Solution: Eliminate extra holes   **Alarm:**

Key Improvement: Part modified to guarantee correct positioning

Description of Process: Plugs are inserted into holes in a circuit board.

Before Improvement:

There were extra holes next to the correct plug holes on the circuit board. Plugs were inserted into them by mistake.

After Improvement:

The extra holes were eliminated. Improper insertion of plugs is completely eliminated.

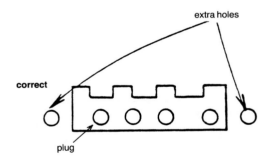

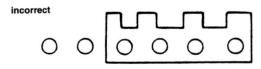

● *Example 144*

Process: Mounting ICs

Problem: ICs inserted backwards

Solution: Make ICs asymmetrical

Key Improvement: Part modified to guarantee correct positioning

Prevent Error: X

Detect Error:

Shutdown:

Control: X

Alarm:

Description of Process: A number of ICs are inserted into a circuit board.

Before Improvement:

The ICs could be inserted backwards because there were the same number of pins on both sides.

After Improvement:

A small modification was made to the IC, by giving it an additional pin on one side and making a corresponding additional hole in the board. It is now impossible to insert the IC backwards, and defects caused by mistaken insertion no longer occur.

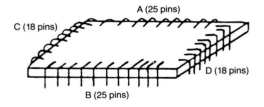

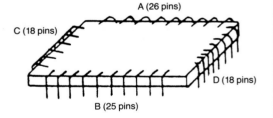

● *Example 145*

Process: Mounting capacitors on circuit boards   **Prevent Error:** X   **Shutdown:**

Problem: Polarity defects   **Detect Error:**   **Control:** X

Solution: Change circuit board design guidelines   **Alarm:**

Key Improvement: Procedure modified to guarantee correct processing

Description of Process: Capacitors are inserted in printed circuit boards.

Before Improvement:

The circuit board designers were free to design the boards as they liked regarding capacitor polarity. The result was that the direction of polarity was completely random. Workers had to exercise extreme vigilance to ensure that capacitors were inserted correctly, but as the number of parts in the circuit boards increased, the incidence of incorrect insertion increased as well.

After Improvement:

The guidelines for circuit board design were changed to require that the polarities of all capacitors are aligned on one axis of the board:
1. the polarities were all aligned on either the X or the Y axis (better);
2. the polarities were all aligned in one direction (best).
Although the result restricts circuit design in some ways, faulty insertion is prevented, and defects are eliminated.

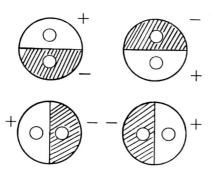

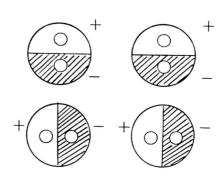

● Example 146

Process: Assembly of cassette deck control buttons   **Prevent Error:** X   **Shutdown:**

Problem: Fast Forward and Rewind buttons reversed   **Detect Error:**   **Control:** X

Solution: Change size of buttons so they are not interchangeable   **Alarm:**

Key Improvement: Part modified to guarantee correct positioning

Description of Process: The control panels of cassette decks are assembled.

Before Improvement:

   The Rewind and the Fast Forward buttons were sometimes mistakenly exchanged during assembly. The buttons had the same size and shape and fit interchangeably. In addition, the symbols on the button are similar.

After Improvement:

   The fact that L1 > L2 was observed. Because of this difference in dimensions, elongating the Rewind button on the left side and elongating the Fast Forward button on the right side prevents the buttons from being mounted in reverse. Mistaken insertion of buttons is completely eliminated.

control panel assembly

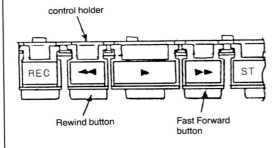

control panel assembly

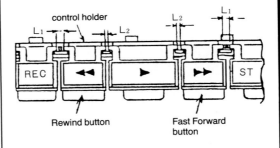

● *Example 147*

Process: Mounting switches on circuit boards

Problem: Switches mounted backwards

Solution: Make switch asymmetrical

Key Improvement: Part modified to guarantee correct positioning

Prevent Error: X

Detect Error:

Shutdown:

Control: X

Alarm:

Description of Process: Switches are mounted in circuit boards.

Before Improvement:

It was difficult to determine the proper mounting direction from the outer appearance of the switch, but the switches had circuit characteristics that were affected by the mounting direction. Defects occurred due to reverse mounting.

After Improvement:

An unneeded switch terminal was cut off and the corresponding hole in the circuit board was eliminated, making it impossible to mount the switch backward. Defects are completely prevented.

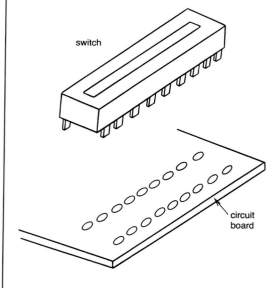

switch

circuit board

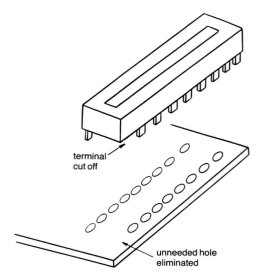

terminal cut off

unneeded hole eliminated

● *Example 148*

Process: Assembly of cassette deck control panels

Problem: Keycaps were mistakenly reversed

Solution: Poka-yoke pins added in different positions to each keycap

Key Improvement: Part modified to guarantee correct positioning

Prevent Error: X

Detect Error:

Shutdown:

Control: X

Alarm:

Description of Process: Keycaps are attached to cassette deck control buttons during control panel assembly. Four kinds of keycaps are bonded to the control buttons.

Before Improvement:

The keycaps and control buttons all had the same shape and were interchangeable. Correct assembly relied exclusively on worker vigilance.

After Improvement:

Poka-yoke pins were added in different positions to each keycap, and matching holes were added to the control buttons. Errors are completely eliminated. This solution can be applied in the future to new models of similar products.

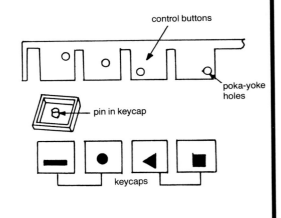

● *Example 149*

Process:　Mounting plates to shafts

Problem:　Plates mounted on wrong end of shaft

Solution:　Add detecting guide to next process

Key Improvement:　Jig modified to detect defective parts

Prevent Error:

Detect Error:　X

Shutdown:

Control:　X

Alarm:

Description of Process:　Plates are mounted onto the ends of shafts.

Before Improvement:

　It was possible to mount the plates to either end of the shafts, resulting in defective parts. These parts often passed down the line unnoticed.

correct

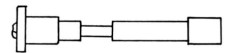

wrong

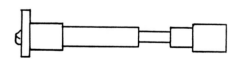

After Improvement:

　A guide was added to the adjusting jig in the next process to detect shafts with the plates on the wrong end. Backward mounted shafts are no longer passed on to later processes.

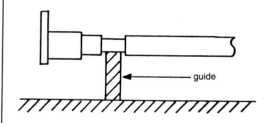

guide

● *Example 150*

Process: Press-fitting parts onto shafts

Problem: Parts were mounted upside down

Solution: Use small difference between top and bottom part dimensions to detect incorrect mounting

Key Improvement: Tool modified to guarantee correct positioning

Prevent Error: X

Detect Error:

Shutdown: X

Control:

Alarm:

Description of Process: A globe-shaped part is mounted onto a shaft by press-fitting.

Before Improvement:

The part is shaped symmetrically on top and bottom, and the end to be fitted to the shaft is almost the same size as the opposite end. Sometimes the parts were fitted onto the shaft upside down. The operator checked during the operation that the part was mounted correctly, but parts were still sometimes mounted upside down, resulting in problems in the following processes.

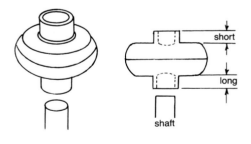

After Improvement:

A detector was devised to alert the operator when a part has been mounted backwards, using the slight difference in lengths of the top and bottom. When a part is mounted backwards (with the longer part at the top), it forces the weight up, spreading the plate spring and releasing the cylinder from the press collet. The press cannot be used for pressing until it is set up again, so incorrect mounting is always noticed by the operator.

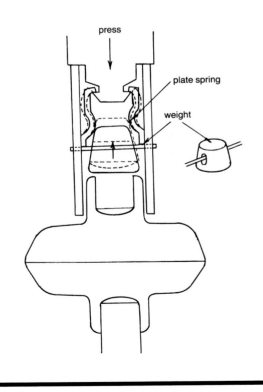

● *Example 151*

Process: Mounting components on circuit boards	**Prevent Error:** X	**Shutdown:**
Problem: Polarity defects	**Detect Error:**	**Control:** X
Solution: Make parts asymmetrical		**Alarm:**

Key Improvement: Part modified to guarantee correct positioning

Description of Process: Electronic parts are inserted into printed circuit boards and soldered. Almost all the electronic parts have polarities. If they are mounted with the wrong polarity, they will not operate correctly.

Before Improvement:

It was possible to mount many of the parts backwards. If insertion errors were discovered at inspection, the parts had to be removed and resoldered. This entailed considerable time and expense.

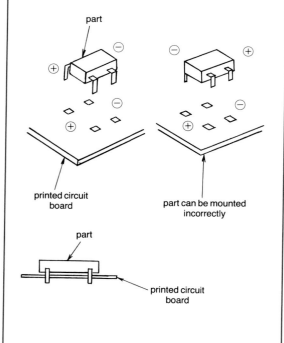

After Improvement:

The key to improvement is to make it impossible to mount the parts with the wrong polarity. Several strategies may be used. If the legs of the part are made different lengths and corresponding holes are made in the mounting jig, the part cannot be mounted backwards. Another method is to vary the spacing between the legs and the holes in the circuit board so that the part fits into the holes in only one orientation.

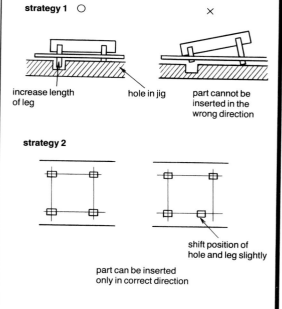

● *Example 152*

Process: Roller bearing assembly

Problem: Omitted rollers

Solution: Count rollers with proximity switch

Key Improvement: Tool modified to detect defective parts

Prevent Error:

Detect Error: X

Shutdown:

Control:

Alarm: X

Description of Process: About twenty rollers are inserted into bearing bodies in the bearing assembly process.

Before Improvement:

Sometimes the roller inserting machine malfunctioned and a few rollers were omitted from a bearing. Bearings with missing rollers went on to later processes. These bearings were sometimes found in visual checks during subsequent processes but sometimes were missed.

After Improvement:

The roller inserting machine has a position where the parts are rotated. A small proximity switch mounted at this position detects the rollers one by one. The signals from the switch are detected and correlated with a time signal. If no roller is detected over a certain interval, an alarm signals a missing roller.

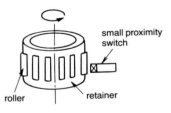

small proximity switch

roller   retainer

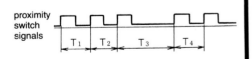

proximity switch signals

T_1 T_2 T_3 T_4

T_3 signals a missing roller

● *Example 153*

Process: Press-fitting steering wheel spoke reinforcement plates

Problem: Plates installed in wrong position

Solution: Jig to prevent faulty positioning

Key Improvement: Jig modified to guarantee correct positioning

Prevent Error: X

Detect Error:

Shutdown:

Control: X

Alarm:

Description of Process: Reinforcement plates are press-fitted into steering wheel spokes.

Before Improvement:

The reinforcement plates sometimes were not pressed into the proper position, and then the spokes could not be mounted correctly.

After Improvement:

The end of the spoke was mounted on a jig equipped with a contact switch at the proper final position of the reinforcement plate. A buzzer sounds and a light goes on to show when the plate has been pressed all the way to the proper position. Faulty positioning is completely eliminated.

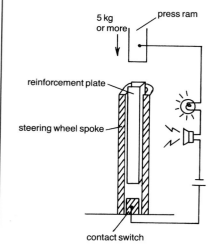

Assembly Omissions

● *Example 154*

Process: Camera case assembly

Problem: Missing camera strap rings

Solution: Microswitch and air cylinder automatically detect missing rings before final inspection.

Key Improvement: Tool used to detect defective parts

Prevent Error:

Detect Error: X

Shutdown:

Control: X

Alarm:

Description of Process: Rings for camera straps are mounted at one point in the camera assembly process.

Before Improvement:

Because the suspension rings have no effect on the functions of the camera, it was impossible to discover their omission in the purely functional intermediate inspections. Instead, the operator mounting the rings made a visual check that the work was correct, then passed the unit on to the next process. Checking errors sometimes occurred, and the omission was often not discovered until the final inspection of the camera's external appearance.

correct

suspension ring

defective

After Improvement:

The visual check for the rings was discontinued in favor of a method using a microswitch and air cylinder. The checking device is mounted on the inspection table, and detection is performed automatically as part of the inspection procedure.

correct

defective

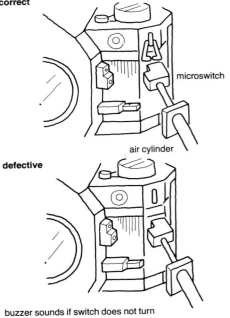

microswitch

air cylinder

buzzer sounds if switch does not turn on within two seconds after timer-controlled air cylinder is actuated

● *Example 155*

Process: Welding nuts to plates

Problem: Omitted nuts

Solution: Detect omission with jig of next process

Key Improvement: Tool modified to detect defective parts

Prevent Error:

Detect Error: X

Shutdown: X

Control:

Alarm:

Description of Process: Two nuts are welded to a part that is then sent on to a panel clamping process.

Before Improvement:

The operators visually checked to see that the nuts had been mounted. However, the operators occasionally allowed parts without nuts to get by.

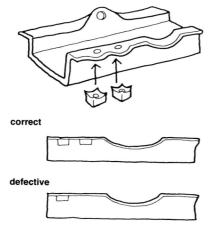

correct

defective

After Improvement:

Limit switches for detecting the nuts are mounted on the jig used in the panel clamp process that followed. The panel clamp does not operate unless both nuts are present, and parts without nuts are no longer sent on to later processes.

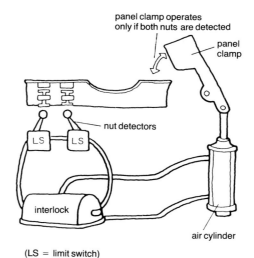

panel clamp operates only if both nuts are detected

panel clamp

nut detectors

LS   LS

interlock

air cylinder

(LS = limit switch)

● *Example 156*

Process: Motorcycle clutch assembly	**Prevent Error:**	**Shutdown:**
Problem: Pushrod ball omitted	**Detect Error:**　X	**Control:**
Solution: Limit switch/air cylinder detector		**Alarm:**　X

Key Improvement: Tool modified to detect defective parts

Description of Process: One of the processes in assembling motorcycle engines is to mount a ball and pushrod for engaging the clutch.

Before Improvement:

Omission of the ball was not always detected by the operators in the subsequent processes, and complaints were received from down the line.

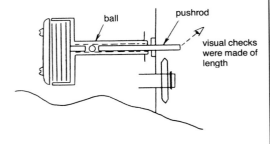

After Improvement:

The pushrod has a different height depending on whether the ball has been inserted or not. This fact was used to develop a simple sensor to detect the omission of the balls. When the ball has been inserted properly, the clamp plate does not tilt and so does not press against the limit switch. On the other hand, if the ball has been omitted, the clamp plate tilts and presses against the limit switch, activating a buzzer alarm.

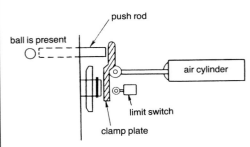

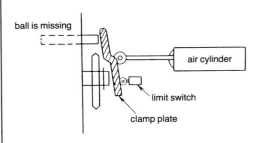

● *Example 157*

Process: Assembling several parts onto a shaft

Problem: Parts omitted

Solution: Automated parts boxes

Key Improvement: Selection of parts automated

Prevent Error: X

Detect Error:

Shutdown:

Control: X

Alarm:

Description of Process: Several parts are assembled onto a shaft. The sequence for assembly is:
1. Take out and mount collar
2. Take out and mount sprocket
3. Mount spring washer
4. Tighten nut

Before Improvement:

The operator sometimes forgot to mount the collar.

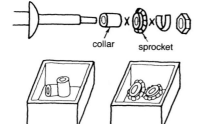

After Improvement:

Automatic parts boxes were developed, controlled by photoelectric detectors. The lid of the sprocket box does not open until the light beam over the collar box has been broken, signaling that the operator has removed a collar. In turn, once the sprocket box is open, the lid of the collar box will not re-open for the next shaft assembly until the light beam over the sprocket box has been broken.

If the operator forgets to mount the collar, the lid of the sprocket box does not open, and the operator realizes the mistake.

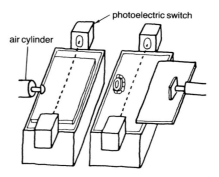

● *Example 158*

Process: Assembling motorcycle engines

Problem: Missing or untightend crankcase bolts

Solution: Automatic tester, using rods and limit switches

Key Improvement: Tool used to detect defective parts

Prevent Error:

Detect Error: X

Shutdown:

Control:

Alarm: X

Description of Process: In motorcycle engine assembly, crankcase bolts are inserted by an operator and tightened by an automated machine.

Before Improvement:

The crankcase continued to move down the line, whether or not the operator inserted the bolts or the machine tightened them. Visual checks and other tests were performed to discover these abnormal items. Because this resulted in the performance of unnecessary operations, it led to increased work-hours and burdened the operators.

After Improvement:

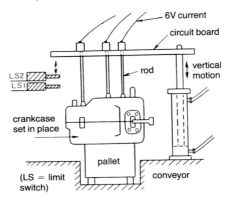

A device was developed to test automatically for missing or untightened bolts. The device has several rods mounted to a circuit board, and the whole assembly is moved up and down with a pneumatic cylinder. The number and position of the rods correspond to those of the bolts.

In use, the rods are supplied with 6V. The device can distinguish between three states:

1. When the bolts are inserted correctly and tightened, the rods contact the bolts (and allow current to flow between the rods) at the same time that limit switches 1 and 2 are actuated by the positioning of the circuit board assembly.

2. If the bolts have not been tightened, current flows through the rods before the circuit board has come into position to actuate the switches.

3. If the bolts have not been inserted, current will not flow even after switch 1 has been actuated by the circuit board.

With this device in use, the number of workhours required for checks is reduced and defective items are no longer sent on to the subsequent processes.

● *Example 159*

Process: Assembly of many different parts   **Prevent Error:**   **Shutdown:**

Problem: Omission of parts   **Detect Error:**   X   **Control:**

Solution: Visual confirmation that all parts have been mounted   **Alarm:**   X

Key Improvement: Procedure modified to guarantee correct processing

Description of Process: Twenty or more parts are mounted in an assembly process.

Before Improvement:

The parts were alphabetically referenced and mounted in that order, but it was difficult for the operator to remember which parts had been mounted, and omissions still tended to occur.

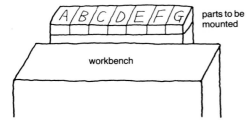

parts to be mounted

workbench

After Improvement:

An "informative" parts container was developed. When each part is taken, the movement of the lid trips a photoelectric switch that turns off a signal lamp. If any light is still on when the operator has finished the assembly, it indicates that some part has been omitted.

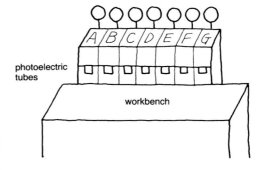

photoelectric tubes

workbench

● Example 160

Process:	A varied series of operations on a single workpiece	**Prevent Error:** X	**Shutdown:**
Problem:	Nuts not tightened	**Detect Error:**	**Control:**
Solution:	Set a timer on the impact wrench		**Alarm:** X

Key Improvement: Procedure modified to guarantee correct processing

Description of Process: Two nuts are tightened as part of a series of operations including setting the welding jig in place and performing the welding.

Before Improvement:

Because the work sites and the amount of work required varied depending on the type of part, the operators sometimes forgot to tighten the nuts.

After Improvement:

A timer connected to the impact wrench used for tightening the nuts is set at X minutes and actuated as soon as the part arrives and is set in place. If the impact wrench has not been used within the set time, a rotating alarm light turns on and a buzzer rings to alert the operator that the nuts must be tightened.

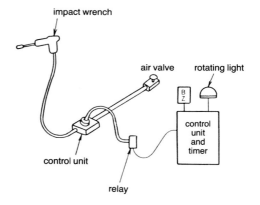

● *Example 161*

Process: Mounting brackets on car floors

Problem: Brackets omitted

Solution: Detect omission of bracket with limit switch in next process

Key Improvement: Jig modified to detect defective parts

Prevent Error:

Detect Error: X

Alarm: X

Shutdown:

Control:

Description of Process: Brackets are mounted on the rear side of the car floor.

Before Improvement:

The operators in the following processes were relied on to determine if the required bracket was missing. The bracket is difficult to check for because of its location on the rear side of the floor, and as a result items with missing brackets were often sent on to the next process.

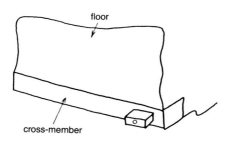

After Improvement:

An air-operated limit switch was installed to determine if the bracket is in place. The air circuit opens as soon as the part is delivered and set into position. If the limit switch does not detect the bracket, it sounds a whistle to alert the operator.

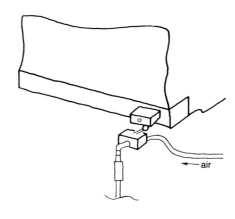

● *Example 162*

Process: Assembly line

Problem: Omitted items

Solution: Detect omissions with limit switches

Key Improvement: Procedure modified to detect defective parts

Prevent Error:

Detect Error: X

Shutdown: X

Control:

Alarm:

Description of Process: Rectangular blocks are mounted on the workpieces, then the workpieces are sent on to subsequent processes.

Before Improvement:

Sometimes the operator forgot to install the blocks. These defects were not detected until the final assembly inspection.

After Improvement:

Two limit switches were installed on the line to detect the presence of the square blocks. The conveyor stops if one switch turns on and the other does not. This completely eliminates omissions during assembly.

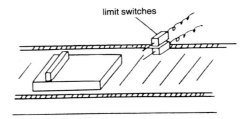

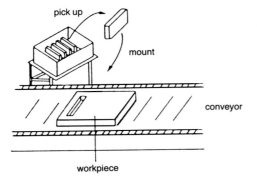

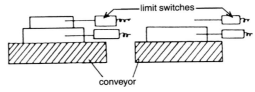

● *Example 163*

Process: Assembly

Problem: Missing parts

Solution: Count parts to make sure the right number have been installed

Key Improvement: Number of parts used compared with number of parts required

Prevent Error:

Detect Error: X

Shutdown:

Control: X

Alarm:

Description of Process: In the assembly process there are several parts, such as small gears, that are mounted behind other parts.

Before Improvement:

Because the parts were hidden, it was difficult to determine if they actually were there and not omitted. Often detection was possible only by dismantling the unit. Workers in previous processes where the small parts were still visible were supposed to check that the parts were installed. However, the check was often overlooked, and products with missing parts were sent on, and some even were sent out onto the market.

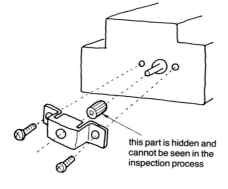

this part is hidden and cannot be seen in the inspection process

After Improvement:

The parts that will be necessary for a given run of products are counted out beforehand and given to the worker. If some of the parts are still on hand after the planned number of products have been assembled, or if there are not enough parts, it is immediately clear that there is an abnormality. This method of checking prevents units with missing parts from being sent out onto the market.

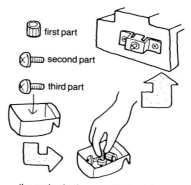

first part
second part
third part

the worker is given exactly the right number for the number of products to be made

● *Example 164*

Process: Assembly

Problem: Omitted items

Solution: Automatic parts boxes interlocked with line movement

Key Improvement: Selection of parts automated

Prevent Error: X

Detect Error:

Shutdown: X

Control:

Alarm: X

Description of Process: The operator mounts a set of parts onto a workpiece on an assembly line.

Before Improvement:

Correct assembly relied entirely on worker vigilance. If the worker was fatigued or stepped away from the line for a moment, some of the parts in the set were often omitted.

After Improvement:

Special parts containers were made to prevent operators from omitting parts during assembly. When the worker opens the lid and takes out a part, a limit switch is actuated and a light is turned on. A stopper on the line allows the part to move to the next station only after all the appropriate lights have turned on (or all the parts have been assembled). This completely eliminates defective units with missing parts.

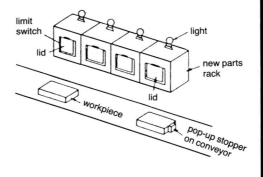

● *Example 165*

Process: Assembling fans

Problem: Omitted parts

Solution: Improve parts storage system

Key Improvement: Selection of parts automated

Prevent Error: X

Detect Error:

Shutdown:

Control: X

Alarm:

Description of Process: Fan blades are assembled onto fan bodies for mounting onto final products.

Before Improvement:

The parts needed to assemble the fan were placed on the workbench and the workers would use them in their assembling sequence. The workers sometimes forgot to mount some of the parts, such as the spring washers or plain washers. The fans were then installed in the products without these parts.

After Improvement:

A rack was developed in which the parts are stored in the order they are used in the assembly process. The parts are accessible through a window on the back edge of the workbench, which moves on rails to allow the worker to take each part out as he or she needs it.

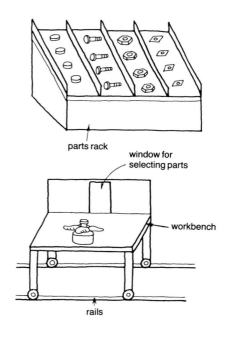

parts rack

window for selecting parts

workbench

rails

● *Example 166*

Process: Mounting shafts to rotors

Problem: Omitting spring washer

Solution: Modify wrench so nut cannot be tightened if washer is missing

Key Improvement: Tool modified to guarantee correct processing

Prevent Error: X

Detect Error:

Shutdown:

Control: X

Alarm:

Description of Process: Shafts are mounted onto rotors with a spring washer and nut, tightened by an automatic torque wrench.

Before Improvement:

The nut could be tightened onto the shaft even if the spring washer was missing. It was not possible to detect the omission after the nut was tightened.

After Improvement:

The screw tip of the torque wrench was improved by shortening it. Missing spring washers can now be detected because without them the nut cannot be tightened and the automatic wrench idles.

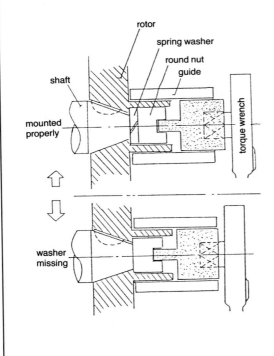

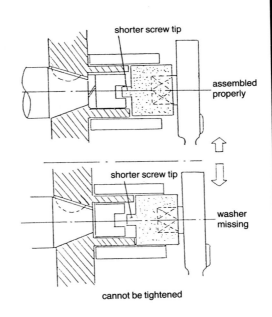

● *Example 167*

Process: Inserting parts during die casting

Problem: Omission of insert parts

Solution: Detect omission of insert electronically in later process

Key Improvement: Tool modified to detect defective parts

Prevent Error:

Detect Error: X

Shutdown: X

Control:

Alarm: X

Description of Process: A certain part is inserted during the die casting process.

Before Improvement:

Because the insert is so critical to the correct operation of the part, 100 percent of the die-cast products were inspected visually and marked with a check. Despite this extensive inspection, customers still complained that insert parts had been omitted.

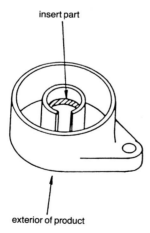

insert part

exterior of product

After Improvement:

A sensor to detect the insert was mounted in the die for the deburring process that follows die casting. The detector is interlocked with the press controls so the press will not operate if the insert is missing. In addition, a signal light and an alarm buzzer are triggered to inform the operator that the part is defective. The visual inspection process has been eliminated, and all defective parts are now detected.

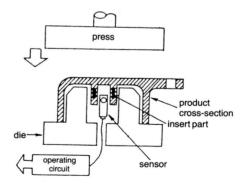

press

product cross-section

insert part

die

operating circuit

sensor

● *Example 168*

Process: Mounting E-rings on rods

Problem: Omission of E-rings

Solution: Use automatic inspection

Key Improvement: Tool used to detect defective parts

Prevent Error:

Detect Error: X

Shutdown:

Control: X

Alarm:

Description of Process: E-rings are mounted on rods.

Before Improvement:

After the rings were mounted, they were checked visually. However, omissions were not detected and the parts were assembled into the final product without E-rings.

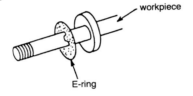

right

wrong

After Improvement:

An automatic detection device was developed, using an air cylinder and a limit switch to detect the presence of the E-ring.

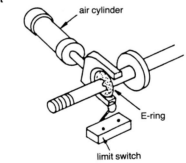

right

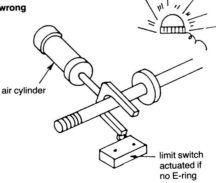

wrong

Processing Omissions

● *Example 169*

Process: Cutting keyways in shaft   **Prevent Error:** X   **Shutdown:** X

Problem: Keyways omitted   **Detect Error:**   **Control:**

Solution: Mounted shaft made unremovable until machine has cut keyway   **Alarm:**

Key Improvement: Tool modified to guarantee correct processing

Description of Process: One operator is responsible for a number of automated oil-hydraulic milling machines, used to cut half-moon-shaped keyways in shafts. The operator sometimes forgets to press the start button on one machine or another. After the keyways are cut, the shafts are heat treated to harden them.

Before Improvement:

Workpieces without keyways were easily mistaken for completed pieces and were taken off the milling machine and sent on the hardening process. However, after the shafts were hardened, they could not be remachined (because of the high degree of hardness) once the missing keyway were discovered. If defective parts were delivered to a customer without being discovered, they were assembled without further checking. Because the keyways were not used until the final process for mounting parts, the defects were not discovered until the very end.

When uncut keyways were discovered at the final process, it was necessary to completely dismantle the parts, which destroyed many of them. Thus, the omission of a keyway had very costly later effects.

After Improvement:

To prevent uncut keyways, an air cylinder and electrical circuit were added to make it impossible to remove the workpiece, once it has been mounted in the milling machine, until the keyway has been cut.

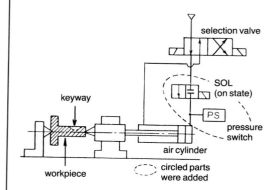

● *Example 170*

Process: Tapping

Problem: Miscounting holes

Solution: Install automatic interlocked counters

Key Improvement: Tool modified to guarantee correct processing count

Prevent Error: X

Detect Error:

Shutdown:

Control: X

Alarm:

Description of Process: Many holes are tapped on each workpiece, using three different sized taps on single-shaft tapping machines. The three processes are:
1. Four M5 through holes are tapped;
2. Two M5 15mm holes are tapped;
3. Three M6 through holes are tapped.

Before Improvement:

The operators counted the holes while tapping, in addition to changing machines after each set of holes. Sometimes holes were not tapped if the operator counted wrong, resulting in situations such as three M5 holes instead of four.

After Improvement:

An electromagnetic counter was attached to each machine. Each counter is set to the proper number of holes to be tapped. When one counter determines that enough holes have been tapped, it turns off its machine and sends a signal to the next machine, allowing it to turn on. When models change it is sufficient to change the counter settings to continue working.

● *Example 171*

Process: Production line

Problem: Unmachined products

Solution: Detect unmachined items by height difference

Key Improvement: Procedure modified to detect defective parts

Prevent Error:

Detect Error: X

Shutdown:

Control:

Alarm: X

Description of Process: A production line sometimes stops temporarily because of machinery troubles or shutdowns.

Before Improvement:

When the production line started again after a shutdown, some of the products moving along the line might not have been machined. The unmachined products passed unnoticed down the line, and these products sometimes broke the dies in following processes.

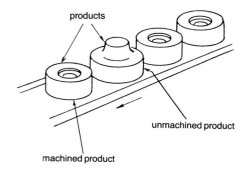

After Improvement:

There is a large difference in height between machined products and those that are not machined. A limit switch was mounted on a gate over the line to detect overheight items. When the limit switch is actuated, an alarm lamp is lit to alert the operator.

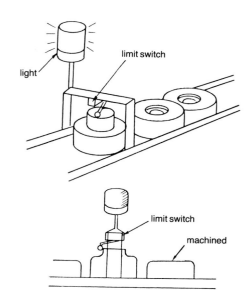

● *Example 172*

Process: Drilling

Problem: Incorrect number of holes

Solution: Counter to count holes drilled

Key Improvement: Tool modified to guarantee correct processing count

Prevent Error: X

Detect Error:

Shutdown: X

Control:

Alarm:

Description of Process: A number of holes are drilled in each workpiece.

Before Improvement:

The operator counted the holes as they were drilled. However, the operator sometimes made errors, and products with the wrong number of holes were produced.

After Improvement:

A counter was mounted on the drill press to detect each hole as it is drilled. Along with this, a limit switch was mounted on the jig to detect when another workpiece has been set in place. These devices are interlocked, and a buzzer sounds if the workpiece is removed and another mounted before the proper number of holes has been drilled.

correct
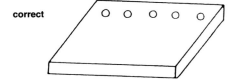

defective
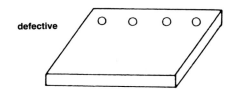

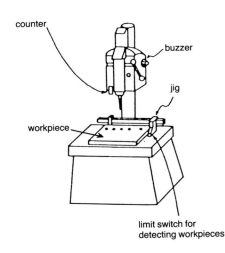

• *Example 173*

Process: Piercing

Problem: Products not pierced

Solution: Detect omission of piercing in next process

Key Improvement: Jig modified to detect defective parts

Prevent Error:

Detect Error: X

Shutdown:

Control: X

Alarm:

Description of Process: Products are die cast and then pierced.

Before Improvement:

Visual checks for piercing were performed in the final inspection before the products were shipped, but customers still discovered some products that had not been completely pierced.

After Improvement:

A pin was mounted on the jig of a process following the die casting, where the part is drilled. If the part has not been pierced, the pin prevents the part from seating correctly on the jig, and omission of piercing is detected. This completely eliminates further processing of unpierced parts.

correct

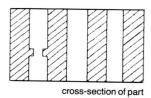

cross-section of part

correct

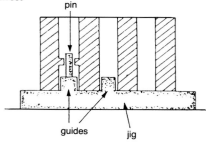

pin

guides   jig

not pierced

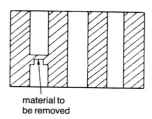

material to
be removed

not pierced

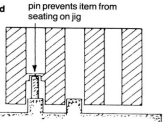

pin prevents item from
seating on jig

● *Example 174*

Process: Drilling

Problem: Drilling omitted

Solution: Install pins in following process to test for drilling

Key Improvement: Tool modified to detect defective parts

Prevent Error: X

Detect Error:

Shutdown:

Control: X

Alarm:

Description of Process: Bearings are drilled, then bent. If the bearings are bent first, it is impossible to drill the holes afterwards.

Before Improvement:

Correct operations relied entirely on worker vigilance. However, workers sometimes inadvertently bent the bearing before they were drilled, creating a defective piece that had to be scrapped.

incorrect sequence

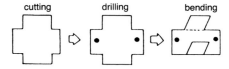

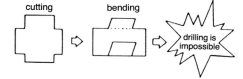

After Improvement:

Pins were added to the bending die, making it impossible to set the bearings in place before they are drilled. Drilling omissions are completely eliminated.

correct sequence

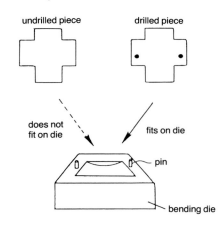

● *Example 175*

Process: Spot welding nuts

Problem: Omission of nuts

Solution: Photoelectric switch detects absence of nut

Key Improvement: Tool modified to guarantee correct processing

Prevent Error: X

Detect Error:

Shutdown: X

Control:

Alarm:

Description of Process: A workpiece and a nut are set on a jig on a spot welding machine and welded together.

Before Improvement:

It was possible to perform the welding if no nut was in place, yielding a defective piece.

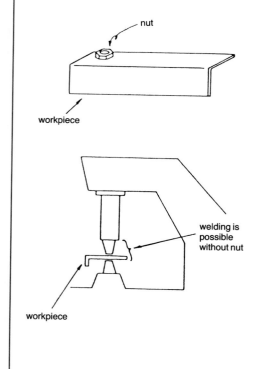

After Improvement:

A photoelectric detector and a light shield were added to the welding machine. If no nut is present on the jig, the welding head lowers the shield through the light beam, and the photoelectric switch turns off the welding machine. If the nut is present, the shield does not interrupt the light beam and welding can proceed.

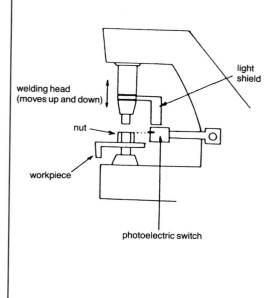

● *Example 176*

Process: Deburring

Problem: Omission of deburring

Solution: Detect remaining burrs in following process

Key Improvement: Tool modified to detect defective parts

Prevent Error:

Detect Error: X

Shutdown:

Control: X

Alarm:

Description of Process: Brackets are cast, deburred, and then drilled.

Before Improvement:

Workers sometimes forget to deburr the brackets. Workpieces were sent on to be drilled even if they had not been deburred, and the defect was not discovered.

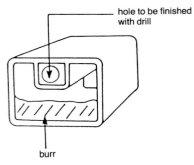

hole to be finished with drill

burr

After Improvement:

A pin to detect remaining burrs was mounted on the drill press head so the drill cannot descend if there are burrs. Deburring omissions are always detected.

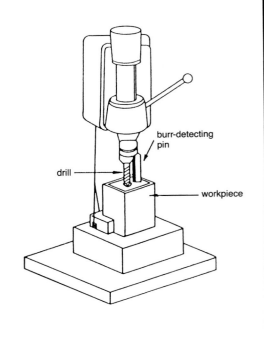

burr-detecting pin

drill

workpiece

● *Example 177*

Process: Inspection	**Prevent Error:**	**Shutdown:**
Problem: Inspection labels omitted	**Detect Error:** X	**Control:**
Solution: Testing jig for detecting presence of labels		**Alarm:** X
Key Improvement: Tool used to detect defective parts		

Description of Process: The worker responsible for testing hose assemblies for pressure-resistance attaches inspection labels after the inspections and then packs the products into boxes.

Before Improvement:

Correct labeling depended on the worker's vigilance, and the labels were sometimes omitted.

inspection label

labeled product

After Improvement:

A jig was developed that tests for the presence of labels. A circuit on the jig is activated when a workpiece is placed on it. If there is no label on the workpiece, current passes through it and a buzzer sounds to alert the worker. If a workpiece is not set in place within a certain time, an alarm interlocked with the line speed rings to prevent omissions of testing.

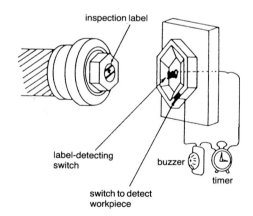

inspection label

label-detecting switch

buzzer

timer

switch to detect workpiece

● *Example 178*

Process: Milling

Problem: Omission of milling

Solution: Modify jig in subsequent process to detect omission of milling

Key Improvement: Tool modified to detect defective parts

Prevent Error:

Detect Error: X

Shutdown:

Control: X

Alarm:

Description of Process: There are three milling processes on a processing line. Workers sometimes omit these processes inadvertently.

Before Improvement:

Workpieces with omitted milling were sent down the line and were eventually made into finished products. The defects were discovered only at the final assembly inspection.

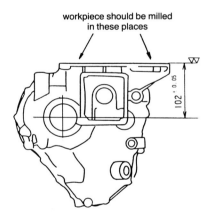

workpiece should be milled in these places

102 ± 0.05

After Improvement:

The jig on the multispindle drilling machine in the process following the milling was improved by adding two bolts, making it impossible to mount workpieces that have not been machined properly.

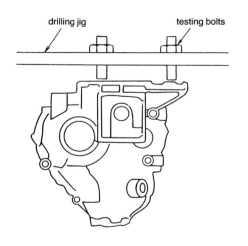

drilling jig   testing bolts

● *Example 179*

Process: Spot welding

Problem: Omission of welds

Solution: Electronic counter

Key Improvement: Tool modified to guarantee correct processing

Prevent Error: X

Detect Error:

Shutdown:

Control: X

Alarm: X

Description of Process: Spot welding is performed on a number of different components. Each component requires a large number of welds.

Before Improvement:

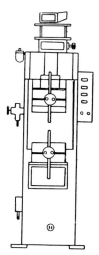

spot welding machine

Operations were carried out by following a work instruction sheet for the welding conditions of the piece to be welded, the number of welds required, etc. Each worker was responsible for remembering the number of welds. Their memories sometimes varied as to the number, and welds were sometimes omitted. If the omitted welds were not discovered in subsequent processes, the defective items went on to the assembly line.

The workers also counted the number of items processed, and if the items were put onto a pallet, time was required to check the number again.

After Improvement:

A digital counter was added to the spot welding machine. The worker sets the required number of welds on the counter, which then counts the welds as they are made. The weld counter is interlocked wih the foot switch used by the operator to perform the welds.

Specifications of the counter panel include the following:

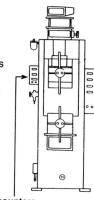

counters

1. One digital preset counter for counting the number of items processed;
2. One or two buzzers, set for the number of each type of weld (some models have two series of welds);
3. A snap switch, display lights, etc., for setting the number of itmes to be processed and the number of welds on each item.

If fifty items are to be processed and each piece has ten welds, a buzzer rings after the tenth weld, and the item counter is incremented. The weld counter is reset automatically. The spot welding machine shuts down after fifty pieces have been processed. In cases where there are two series of welds on the same item, both numbers are input to the weld counter, and then output to the item counter.

Welds are no longer omitted. The worker no longer needs to count the number of welds, and the count of items processed is much more accurate. The amount of work completed can be checked at any time.

● *Example 180*

Process: Drilling

Problem: Holes not drilled

Solution: Improve next jig to detect omissions

Key Improvement: Jig modified to detect defective parts

Prevent Error:

Detect Error: X

Shutdown:

Control: X

Alarm:

Description of Process: As a result of design changes, after several holes are drilled in an automatic process, additional holes are drilled manually.

Before Improvement:

The additional holes were sometimes omitted.

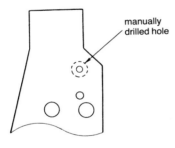

manually drilled hole

After Improvement:

The jig in the next process was modified with a pin to detect omitted holes. Omissions are always detected.

additional pin on jig in next process detects workpieces with drilling omitted

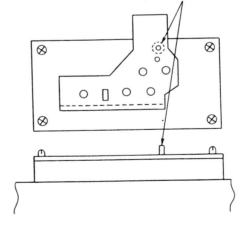

● *Example 181*

Process: Tapping

Problem: Tapping omitted and operator errors

Solution: Switch to detect successful tapping

Key Improvement: Tool modified to guarantee correct processing

Prevent Error: X

Detect Error:

Shutdown:

Control: X

Alarm:

Description of Process: A tapping machine is in continuous use. A counter registers each tapping, and the number of taps is compared to the number of items to be tapped.

Before Improvement:

The counter registered each attempt to tap a workpiece, whether the attempt was successful or not. Operator errors and blank strikes were counted, and many untapped or incompletely tapped items were mixed with the properly finished items.

After Improvement:

A detection switch was installed in connection with a plate cam attached to the tapping machine shaft. The switch is interlocked into the tapping machine mechanism, so that the tap head can rise only if it has been moved all the way into operating position and the motor has run long enough for the tapping to be successful.

Untapped items are completely eliminated. This improvement can be applied to other drilling or tapping processes.

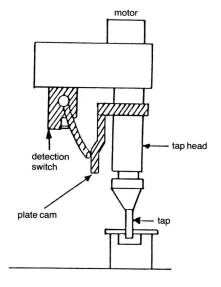

motor

detection switch

plate cam

tap head

tap

● *Example 182*

Process: Cutting grooves in long rods

Problem: Grooves omitted

Solution: Detect omissions by comparison with correctly machined parts

Key Improvement: Template used for inspection

Prevent Error:

Detect Error: X

Shutdown:

Control: X

Alarm:

Description of Process: Long rods are mounted in a lathe and grooves are cut at various positions along their lengths.

Before Improvement:

The machined rods were checked individually, but often this took too many workhours. Machining was sometimes omitted inadvertently, and the un-machined items would be overlooked and sent on to the next process, where they could not be installed.

correctly machined

defective item   missing groove

After Improvement:

The rods are placed in a specially built sorting box to be compared after machining. Any omission of machining is distinguished at a glance.

item with missing groove is immediately obvious

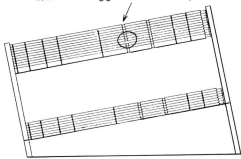

● *Example 183*

Process: Drilling

Problem: Drilling omitted

Solution: Direct comparison using correctly processed item as a template

Key Improvement: Template used for inspection

Prevent Error:

Detect Error: X

Shutdown:

Control: X

Alarm:

Description of Process: Many holes are drilled in the workpieces in a sequence of a several different processes.

Before Improvement:

Visual checks for omissions were made by comparing the workpieces with a drawing. However, this method required too many workhours, and it was easy to overlook omissions. Defective items were sent on to the next process where they could not be installed.

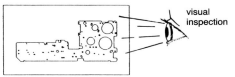

drawing of completed product

visual inspection

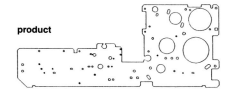

product

After Improvement:

A properly processed sample product is used as a template to determine if any holes have been omitted. The worker lays the template on top of the completed product and shines a light through from below. It is possible to distinguish defective items at a glance, and mistakes in checking have been completely eliminated.

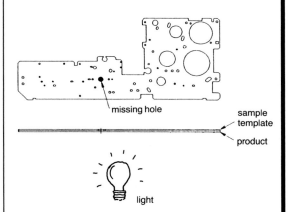

missing hole

sample template

product

light

● *Example 184*

Process: Drilling

Problem: Drilling omitted after model changeover

Solution: Improve jig in next process to detect omissions

Key Improvement: Jig modified to detect defective parts

Prevent Error:

Detect Error: X

Shutdown:

Control: X

Alarm:

Description of Process: Two models use similar parts, but for one model the part has holes, and for the other model the part has no holes. For one model, the part passes through cutting, drilling, and pressing processes, and for the other model the part is cut and pressed but not drilled.

Before Improvement:

Because of misunderstandings and confusion, the operator sometimes omitted the drilling process in the part requiring drilling.

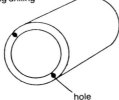
part requiring drilling

hole

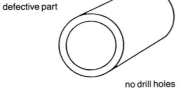
defective part

no drill holes

After Improvement:

Because the press jig is changed for each model, detecting pins were installed on the press jig for the part requiring drilling. It is impossible to press items that have not been drilled, and defective items have been completely eliminated.

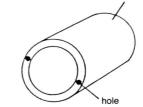
part requiring drilling

hole

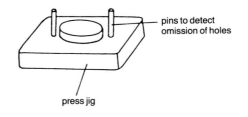
pins to detect omission of holes

press jig

● *Example 185*

Process:　Tapping

Problem:　Tapping omitted

Solution:　Count number of taps performed

Key Improvement:　Tool modified to guarantee correct processing

Prevent Error:　X

Detect Error:

Shutdown:

Control:　X

Alarm:

Description of Process: In a process where parts are manufactured for several different models, about ten holes are tapped on each workpiece, using a single-spindle drill press.

Before Improvement:

　　The operators checked the positions and number of holes as they worked. However, this control relied strictly on the workers' vigilance and tapping was omitted now and then.

After Improvement:

　　A counter was added to the tapping machine. The operator clears the counter for each workpiece and checks that the number of taps is correct for the current model. Although this amounts only to a method for assisting the vigilance of the operator, it almost completely eliminates omissions of tapping.

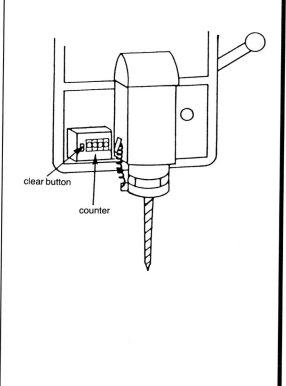

clear button

counter

● *Example 186*

Process: Pressing

Problem: Pressing omitted

Solution: Finished part delivery chute will not accept unprocessed parts

Key Improvement: Chute modified to sort out defective parts

Prevent Error:

Detect Error: X

Shutdown:

Control: X

Alarm:

Description of Process: The insert portion of a part is pressed to create the finished shape.

Before Improvement:

The operator stood facing the press, feeding the unprocessed items from the left and placing the finished items in a bin on the right side. Because of confusion when laying out the parts, or when operations were interrupted by rest periods or the like, the pressing was sometimes omitted and unprocessed items were placed on the table with the finished items. Defective items were often not discovered until final inspection before shipment.

finished item

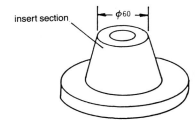

insert section — φ60

unprocessed item

φ66

After Improvement:

A chute was devised to carry the finished parts to a delivery box. The insert section of a correctly processed item fits in the chute and the part slides to the box, but an unprocessed item will not fit. Because the operator can easily detect omission of processing, failure to press these parts is completely eliminated.

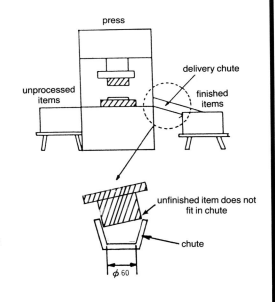

press

unprocessed items

delivery chute

finished items

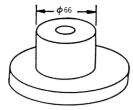

unfinished item does not fit in chute

chute

φ 60

Measurement Errors

● *Example 187*

Process: Packing finished goods into delivery containers

Problem: Containers not filled

Solution: Containers are weighed after packing

Key Improvement: Operation tied to value of critical physical quantity

Prevent Error:

Detect Error: X

Shutdown:

Control:

Alarm: X

Description of Process: Finished gears are packed into containers for delivery to customers.

Before Improvement:

Workers sometimes did not notice gaps between gears in the containers and packed too few items. It was not possible to detect this omission.

After Improvement:

The containers are packed on a scale. If there are too few gears in a box, it will not weigh enough, and the omission is detected.

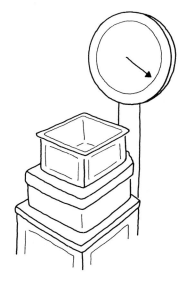

● *Example 188*

Process: Weighing boxes of finished parts

Problem: Weighing was omitted

Solution: Box removable only if weight sufficient

Key Improvement: Operation tied to value of critical physical quantity

Prevent Error: X

Detect Error:

Shutdown:

Control: X

Alarm:

Description of Process: Finished parts are packed into boxes for delivery to the customers. The boxes are packed on a scale, so the workers can determine if the proper number of parts have been packed.

Before Improvement:

The workers checked the weight of the box against a mark at the proper weight on the scale. Sometimes the workers forgot to check, and an incorrectly packed box was delivered to a customer.

After Improvement:

An interference plate was mounted on the base of the scale, and a proximity switch was mounted on the dial. The interference plate prevents the box from being removed from the scale until the limit switch detects the proper weight.

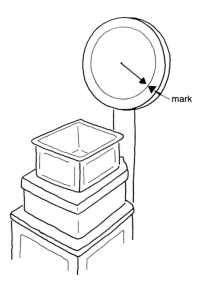

mark

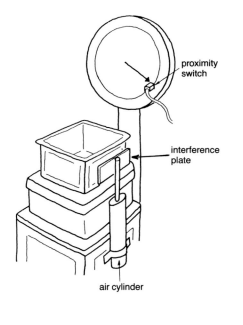

proximity switch

interference plate

air cylinder

● *Example 189*

Process: Packing

Problem: Wrong number of parts packed

Solution: Mechanical counting

Key Improvement: Tool modified to guarantee correct processing

Prevent Error: X

Detect Error:

Shutdown:

Control: X

Alarm:

Description of Process: Washers are packed into delivery boxes by threading twenty-five at a time onto rods, then packing four rods into each box, resulting in 100 washers per box.

Before Improvement:

Sometimes the rods had twenty-four or twenty-six washers threaded on, and the boxes ended up with the wrong number of washers. In addition, the rods were hard to handle when they were loaded with washers.

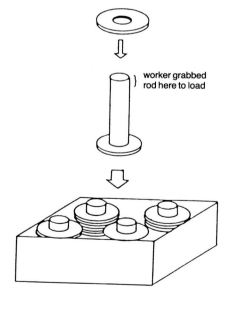

worker grabbed rod here to load

After Improvement:

A mark is made on the rods at the level of the twenty-fifth washer so that too few washers can be detected. The rods were drilled so that a handle with a retaining pin can be inserted. If there are twenty-six washers, the hole will be blocked. The retaining pin thus prevents mistakes in counting the washers and makes the rods easier to handle.

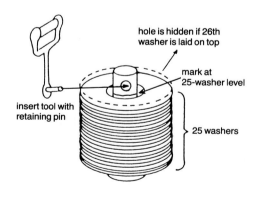

hole is hidden if 26th washer is laid on top

mark at 25-washer level

insert tool with retaining pin

25 washers

● *Example 190*

Process: Packing parts for delivery to succeeding processes

Problem: Wrong number of parts packed/wrong parts packed

Solution: Automated parts rack

Prevent Error: X

Detect Error:

Shutdown:

Control: X

Alarm:

Key Improvement: Selection of parts automated

Description of Process: At a supply depot for a number of different processes, various parts are packed for delivery to the processes. Each process requires a specific number of different parts.

Before Improvement:

For each process, the worker consulted an instruction sheet telling the number and types of parts that should be packed for that process. The worker took the parts from their bins one by one and packed them into boxes. Sometimes the parts were counted incorrectly or the wrong parts were taken inadvertently.

After Improvement:

Two goals were defined: (1) the parts needed and the quantities needed should be indicated mechanically; and (2) there should be a check that the number of parts packed is correct.

A "smart" parts rack was installed to achieve these goals. The worker inserts an instruction card for a given process into a card reader on the rack. A light goes on at the bin of the first part specified. When the worker has taken the correct number of parts, a buzzer sounds and a light goes on at the next part. The worker repeats this procedure for each process.

This new procedure has completely eliminated delivery of the wrong parts or the wrong number of parts and has also tripled the worker's speed.

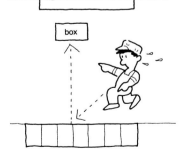

● *Example 191*

Process: Measuring product by weighing

Problem: Weighing errors

Solution: Photoelectric detector for proper weight condition

Key Improvement: Tool modified to guarantee correct processing

Prevent Error: X

Detect Error:

Shutdown:

Control:

Alarm: X

Description of Process: Workers pack a pigment solution into cans by setting the cans on a scale and pouring in the product until the can has the proper amount of product.

Before Improvement:

Workers watched the scale to determine when the can was full. After filling several hundred cans the workers would tire, and weighing errors would result, slowing down the work.

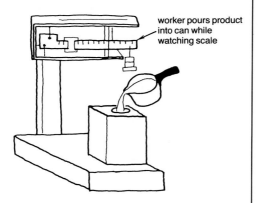

worker pours product into can while watching scale

After Improvement:

A photoelectric detector was installed to monitor the movement of the scale, activating a buzzer when the scale reaches the correct weight. Much less vigilance is required, resulting in less worker fatigue. Weighing errors substantially reduced, and the operating efficiency (per can) is improved.

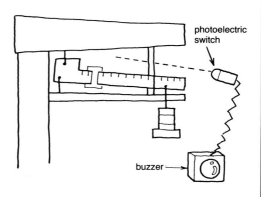

photoelectric switch

buzzer

● *Example 192*

Process: Automatic box packing

Problem: Detecting unfilled boxes

Solution: Blow empty boxes off conveyor belt

Key Improvement: Procedure modified to detect defective parts

Prevent Error:

Detect Error: X

Shutdown:

Control: X

Alarm:

Description of Process: Boxes are filled and closed automatically on a conveyor belt.

Before Improvement:

Sometimes boxes were not filled because of some error in the machinery, but they were closed anyway and delivered along the conveyor.

closed box —
is it empty or full?

After Improvement:

Because the empty boxes are light, they are blown off the conveyor belt with compressed air directed at the boxes from the side.

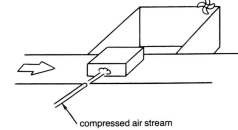

pinwheel indicates air stream

compressed air stream

Dimensional Errors

● *Example 193*

Process: Cutting wire roll stock to length   **Prevent Error:** X   **Shutdown:**

Problem: Incorrect lengths   **Detect Error:**   **Control:** X

Solution: Ensure length is correctly measured   **Alarm:**

Key Improvement: Tool modified to guarantee correct processing

---

Description of Process: Wire roll stock is cut to length in a cutting jig.

Before Improvement:

There were no problems when short lengths of stock were cut, but when long lengths were cut, variations in length appeared, and troubles occurred in later processes.

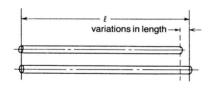

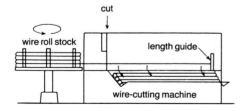

After Improvement:

The variations in length were caused by curvature of the stock or by the stock sagging in the cutting jig. A vertical guide was made that straightens the stock before it is cut. This simple guide completely eliminates length variations.

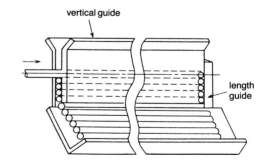

● *Example 194*

Process: Machining round bars

Problem: Incorrect dimensions

Solution: Mechanical detection of machining errors

Key Improvement: Chute modified to detect defective parts

Prevent Error:

Detect Error: X

Shutdown:

Control: X

Alarm:

Description of Process: Steps are machined onto round brass bar stock, to the shape shown in the drawing. Because of possible variations in machining, it is necessary to check the finished dimensions of each step when it is completed.

Before Improvement:

   The dimensions of the bars were checked manually with gages.

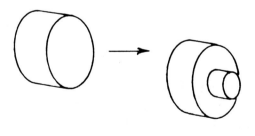

After Improvement:

   An inclined chute with a guide was installed, and the completed bars are rolled along the guide. Interference plates mounted on the guide detect dimensional irregularities in the machined steps.

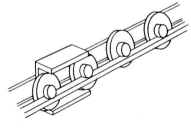

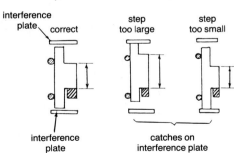

interference plate — correct — step too large — step too small — interference plate — catches on interference plate

● *Example 195*

Process: Sewing buttonholes on men's suits

Prevent Error: X

Shutdown:

Problem: Positions of buttonholes incorrect

Detect Error:

Control: X

Solution: Substitute gage for ruler

Alarm:

Key Improvement: Jig used to guarantee correct positioning

Description of Process: The spacing between buttonholes on men's suits varies depending on the size of the suit.

Before Improvement:

A ruler was used to measure the proper position for the buttonholes, and the positions were marked with chalk. Errors occurred because the workers would accidentally misread the ruler or measure for the wrong size.

After Improvement:

A combination gage including buttonhole-marking gages for sizes 3, 4, 5, and 6 was devised. It is aligned as shown in the drawing when marking the suit for buttonholes. Mismeasurement is eliminated.

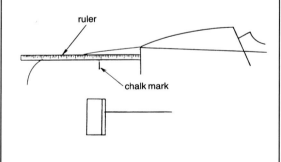

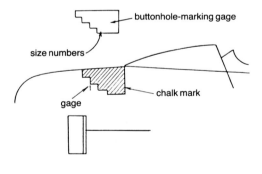

● *Example 196*

Process: Cutting pipes to length

Problem: Pipes cut too short

Solution: Prevent cutting until pipes are properly positioned.

Key Improvement: Tool modified to guarantee correct processing

Prevent Error: X

Detect Error:

Alarm: X

Shutdown: X

Control:

Description of Process: Several pipes are put in a jig against a length guide and cut to length at the same time. Workers adjust the length guide for the different lengths of pipe required.

Before Improvement:

Workers sometimes inadvertently cut the pipes without positioning them in contact with the length guide, and the pipes were cut too short. These pipes could not be used and had to be discarded.

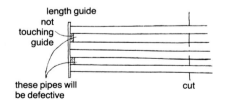

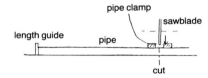

After Improvement:

The length guide was modified with limit switches that sense when each individual pipe is positioned properly, and a shut-off circuit was connected to the cutter switch. The limit switches can be switched out of the shut-off circuit at a control board, so the number of pipes to be cut at a time can be varied. If some of the required limit switches are not actuated, a red light goes on and the cutter switch will not operate. It is impossible to cut pipes if they are not positioned correctly.

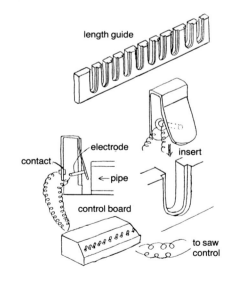

● *Example 197*

Process: Cutting hose to length   **Prevent Error:** X   **Shutdown:**

Problem: Hose cut too long   **Detect Error:**   **Control:**   X

Solution: Ensure hose is stretched tight   **Alarm:**

Key Improvement: Jig modified to guarantee correct positioning

Description of Process: In a small workshop where there is not much room to work, a hardware fitting is attached to the end of a flexible hose which is then pulled around a series of guides and cut to length.

Before Improvement:

   Because the guides had wide grooves, the hose did not always lie straight on the guides and was sometimes cut too long as a result.

After Improvement:

   The guides were modified to taper toward the bottom. When the hose is pulled taut against the guides, it invariably passes through the guides at the right positions, ensuring that the hose is cut at the correct length.

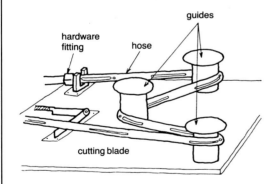

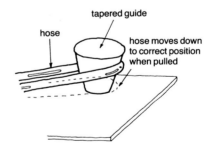

Omissions of Operations

● *Example 198*

Process: Induction hardening   **Prevent Error:** X   **Shutdown:** X

Problem: Cooling water not supplied   **Detect Error:**   **Control:**

Solution: Interlock heating switch to supply of cooling water   **Alarm:**

Key Improvement: Tool modified to protect it from damage

Description of Process: Cooling water to prevent overheating is passed through the heating coils in an induction hardening process. The cooling water is supplied via a stopcock operated by the worker.

Before Improvement:

The operator sometimes forgot to open the stopcock for the cooling water before turning on the heating switch. This resulted in heat damage to the coils and led to accidents.

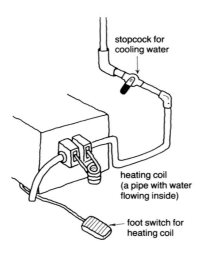

After Improvement:

A limit switch was mounted on the stopcock. If the stopcock is not opened, the heating switch does not turn on.

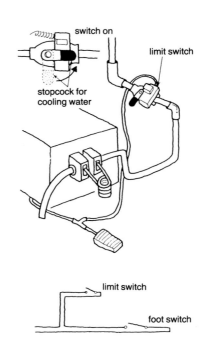

● *Example 199*

Process: Manufacturing pigments

Problem: Solvents not preheated

Solution: Automatic solvent heater operation

Key Improvement: Tool modified to guarantee correct processing

Prevent Error: X

Detect Error:

Shutdown:

Control: X

Alarm:

Description of Process: In a factory manufacturing pigments, some of the solvents must be heated and dissolved before the workers begin work in the morning. The boilers must be turned on two to three hours before starting time.

Before Improvement:

The workers took turns coming to work early to turn on the boiler switches. However, sometimes the worker whose turn it was would forget and the other workers would be kept waiting at starting time, which disrupted the overall operating schedule.

After Improvement:

Electric heaters were mounted on each of the water tanks used for dissolving the solvents. The heaters are equipped with timer switches set to turn on automatically several hours in advance so the solvents are dissolved by starting time. This eliminated the need for a worker to come early, as well as the problem of forgetfulness.

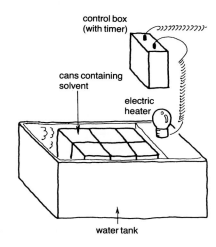

control box
(with timer)

cans containing
solvent

electric
heater

water tank

● *Example 200*

Process: Heating-bonding machine

Problem: Heating switch not turned off

Solution: Heating switch is automatically turned off at the completion of the process

Key Improvement: Tool modified to protect it from damage

Prevent Error: X

Detect Error:

Shutdown: X

Control:

Alarm:

Description of Process: A heating-bonding machine is used to bond together two test pieces. The test pieces are pressed down by the upper head and then heated. After bonding, the head is raised and the heating switch is turned off.

Before Improvement:

Some machines were used by several different people and did not have single operators assigned exclusively to them. The various switches on these machines are sometimes not turned off. Failure to turn off sources of heat is a particularly serious fire hazard. Such errors must be absolutely prevented.

After Improvement:

A boss was mounted on the strut of the upper head. When the head goes all the way up, the boss trips a limit switch, turning off the heating switch. Failure to turn off the heating switch is prevented.

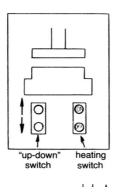

"up-down" switch   heating switch

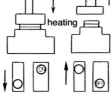

heating

process 1 ⟶ process 2

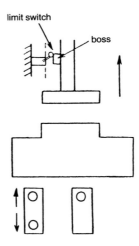

limit switch   boss

● *Example 201*

Process: U-shaped processing line   **Prevent Error:** X   **Shutdown:** X

Problem: Machine operations omitted   **Detect Error:**   **Control:**

Solution: Interlock machines so one process does not start until the preceding operation is started   **Alarm:**

Key Improvement: Jig modified to guarantee correct processing

Description of Process: A worker operates a number of machines arranged into a U-shaped processing line. After setting a workpiece in the jig of one machine and starting the processing there, the worker moves to the next operation, sets it up, and starts it.

Before Improvement:

The worker sometimes forgot to start an operation after setting the workpiece on the jig. Delays or omitted processing resulted.

After Improvement:

Limit switches were mounted on the jigs so the process power circuits can be interlocked. It is now impossible to turn on the switch for one machine until the start button for the preceding operation has been pressed.

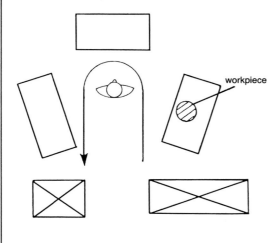

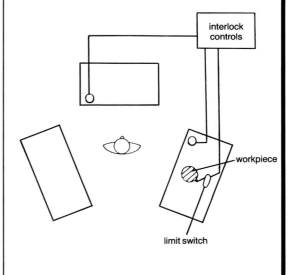

Operations Errors

● *Example 202*

Process: Turning

Problem: Chuck key not removed before operation of the lathe

Solution: Interlock lathe power switch with chuck key storage rack

Key Improvement: Tool modified to protect operator from danger

Prevent Error: X

Detect Error:

Shutdown: X

Control:

Alarm:

Description of Process: Workers chuck workpieces into a metal turning lathe, then return the chuck key to its storage rack before starting the lathe. The worker can be injured if the chuck key is not removed from the chuck before the lathe is started.

Before Improvement:

It was possible to start the lathe while the chuck key was still in the chuck.

After Improvement:

A limit switch was installed in the chuck key storage rack to detect the presence of the chuck key. The limit switch is interlocked with the power switch for the lathe so the lathe cannot be started if the chuck key has not been returned to the rack. In addition, a red lamp comes on when the chuck key is off the storage rack.

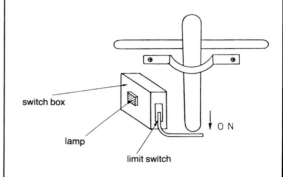

switch box

lamp

limit switch

ON

● *Example 203*

Process: Crane inspection

Problem: Crane could be operated while inspector was on crane

Solution: Interlock crane ladder to operating circuit

Prevent Error: X

Detect Error:

Shutdown: X

Control:

Alarm:

Key Improvement: Tool modified to protect operator from danger

Description of Process: Cranes must be given daily, monthly, and annual inspections. The inspectors work on the crane, using a ladder to climb up onto the crane structure. The other workers cannot see the inspectors when they are on the crane.

Before Improvement:

Operators sometimes started up the crane without realizing that an inspector was at work on it. Fortunately, no accidents resulted, but the situation presented a serious safety risk.

After Improvement:

The ladder used to climb onto the crane has folding rungs, whch are normally raised so no one can climb the crane. However, when the inspector lowers the rungs, a limit switch interlocked with the controls of the crane is tripped, preventing the crane from operating and assuring the inspector's safety.

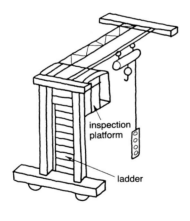

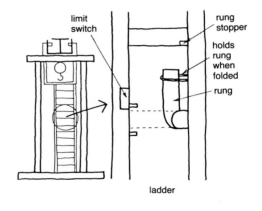

● *Example 204*

Process: Lens rinsing

Problem: Lenses and processing cards mixed up after rinsing

Solution: Color/number-coded rinsing racks and processing cards

Key Improvement: Procedure modified to guarantee correct processing

Prevent Error: X

Detect Error:

Shutdown:

Control: X

Alarm:

Description of Process: Lenses are rinsed ultrasonically in rinsing racks. The lenses each have processing cards to identify them. During rinsing the lenses are separated from their processing cards.

Before Improvement:

After setting the lenses in the rinsing racks, the operator retained their processing cards, put the racks on the entrance belt of the rinsing machine, and filed the processing cards in order on the workbench on the outlet side. After rinsing, the lenses on their rinsing racks were matched with their processing cards. However, lenses were sometimes mismatched when rush orders were being processed or when the lot was handled by more than one operator. This was especially true when many lenses had the same shapes and sizes.

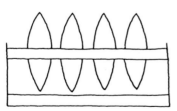

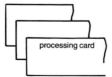

processing card

After Improvement:

Using clips with number plates of different colors, the lenses and processing cards can be tracked through the rinsing process. Several clips are provided for each number, and the cards and rinsing racks are clearly matched, in numerical order, by assigning the same number to each, putting one clip on the rinsing rack and a clip with the same number on the processing card.

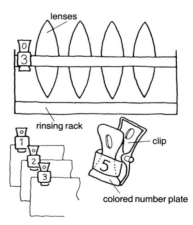

lenses

rinsing rack

clip

colored number plate

● *Example 205*

Process: Automated casting line

Problem: Stopcock for cooling water not opened

Solution: Automatic cooling water supply

Key Improvement: Tool modified to protect it from damage

Prevent Error: X

Detect Error:

Shutdown:

Control: X

Alarm:

Description of Process: On a fully automated casting line using casting robots, each operator is assigned to more than one machine. The dies must be cooled, and the valve for the cooling water must be opened soon after casting begins.

Before Improvement:

At about the third shot after the beginning of casting, the operator was to open the master valve for the water to cool the interior of the die. When the operator forgot to open the valve, problems sometimes ensued, such as the casting sticking to the dies or the dies becoming deformed by the heat.

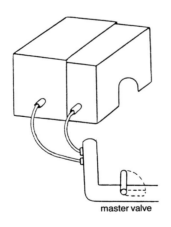
master valve

After Improvement:

A solenoid-controlled valve and a counter were added to the process. The counter counts three shots after the beginning of casting and then signals the solenoid to open the water valve.

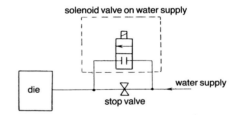
solenoid valve on water supply
die
water supply
stop valve

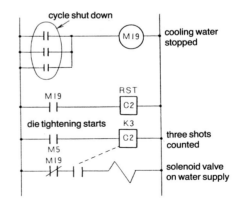
cycle shut down
M19 — cooling water stopped
M19   RST C2
die tightening starts   K3 C2 — three shots counted
M5
M19 — solenoid valve on water supply

● *Example 206*

Process: Metal lathe

Problem: Cooling oil siphoned backward and
spilled on floor

Solution: Prevent siphoning

Key Improvement: Tool modified to protect it from damage

Prevent Error: X

Detect Error:

Shutdown:

Control: X

Alarm:

Description of Process: A pump is used to circulate cooling oil from a reservoir under the numerically controlled lathe and return it to the oil tank.

Before Improvement:

After the lathe and pump were turned off, a siphoning action was produced between the discharge pipe in the oil tank and the lathe reservoir. The oil flowed back in the wrong direction and overflowed onto the floor.

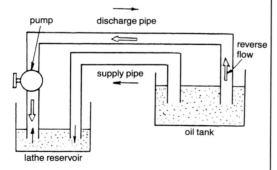

After Improvement:

The discharge pipe was cut shorter so suction can never build up and cause siphoning. Reverse flow and spilling are eliminated.

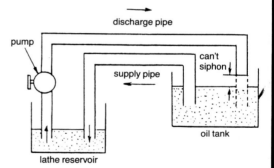

Pasting/Labeling Errors

● *Example 207*

Process: Pasting labels into molded parts   **Prevent Error:** X   **Shutdown:**

Problem: Labels pasted in backwards or upside down   **Detect Error:**   **Control:** X

Solution: Modify the shape of the label and the recess it fits into on the molded part   **Alarm:**

Key Improvement: Part modified to guarantee correct positioning

---

Description of Process: Rating labels are pasted into a recess in a molded chassis.

Before Improvement:

The recess and the label were both rectangular in shape, and the label could be pasted in upside down or backwards.

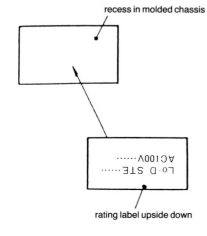

recess in molded chassis

rating label upside down

After Improvement:

A notch was made in the corner of the label, and a corresponding notch was made in the recess of the chassis. The label can be mounted only in the correct orientation, and incorrect mounting is completely eliminated.

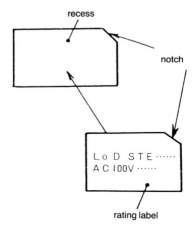

recess

notch

rating label

● *Example 208*

Process: Attaching printed labels to cassette decks   **Prevent Error:** X   **Shutdown:**

Problem: Labels attached upside down   **Detect Error:**   **Control:** X

Solution: Change shape of label and area it is attached to   **Alarm:**

Key Improvement: Part modified to guarantee correct positioning

Description of Process: Labels for the push-button functions are attached to cassette decks.

Before Improvement:

 The label was rectangular and could easily be stuck on upside down by mistake.

REC ◀◀ ◀ ▶▶ STOP PAUSE

After Improvement:

 The shape of the label and the area to which it is attached was modified so the label cannot be attached upside down. Defects are completely eliminated and the design value of the cassette deck is increased.

REC ◀◀ ▶ ▶▶ STOP PAUSE

● *Example 209*

Process: Labeling and stamping products in small lots **Prevent Error:** X **Shutdown:**

Problem: Insufficient setup time, leading to various labeling and stamping quality errors **Detect Error:** **Control:** X

Solution: Vary speed of conveyor so operator can ensure quality **Alarm:**

Key Improvement: Tool modified to guarantee correct processing

Description of Process: The manufacturing line changed from primarily a mass-production facility where packaged parts were marked with labels to primarily small-lot production where the packages can be marked with either labels or stamps. One worker sets up and operates both a labeling machine and a rubber stamp station.

Before Improvement:

No problems occurred in the past when the manufacturing line was used for mass production and only labels were used. As small-lot production increased, errors began to occur in unexpected places. Because packaged parts could be marked either by stamping or by labeling, the number of setup operations increased. This led to errors such as stamps too thinly inked, misaligned labels, and labels pasted with insufficient paste. Time and trouble were required to correct these errors.

After Improvement:

Research showed the problems were caused because the packed boxes were labeled on a conveyor moving at a constant speed, which does not give enough time to change setups. It was determined that the labeling and stamping errors can be eliminated if the speed at which packages are fed into the marking process can be varied. A short conveyor with variable speed controls was installed between the chute and the labeling machine. The operator can make visual checks of the labeling process until it is clear that the stamps are inked sufficiently or that the labels are pasted in the correct position with sufficient paste. The labeling and pasting errors are eliminated.

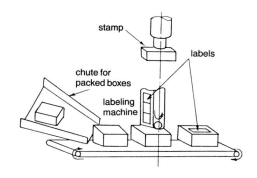

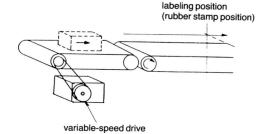

● *Example 210*

Process: Pasting on information plates

Problem: Omission of plates

Solution: Detect missing plates with photoelectric switch

Key Improvement: Tool modified to detect defective parts

Prevent Error:

Detect Error: X

Shutdown:

Control:

Alarm: X

Description of Process: An information plate is pasted onto each product.

Before Improvement:

Workers sometimes forgot to paste on information plates due to miscommunication or interruptions in operation.

After Improvement:

A photoelectric detector was installed to detect the reflective plate on the product. If the plate is not installed, a light goes on and a buzzer rings. This eliminates omissions of the information plates.

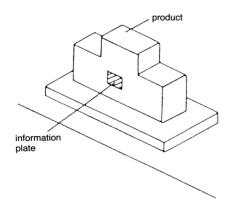

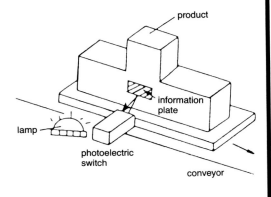

Inspection Errors

● *Example 211*

Process:	Trimming small metal pieces in a punch press	**Prevent Error:**	X	**Shutdown:**	
Problem:	Magnetic detector inaccuracies	**Detect Error:**		**Control:**	X
Solution:	Standardize passage of metal through magnetic detector			**Alarm:**	

Key Improvement: Tool modified to guarantee correct processing

Description of Process: Small metal parts are trimmed in a punch press. After punching, the part is blown out of the die and through a magnetic detector. If the detector confirms that the previous part is out of the die, the press is reloaded and the process begins again.

Before Improvement:

The sensitivity of the magnetic detector varies between the central section and the outer edges. For small, thin parts, the detector cannot be adjusted to detect parts passing through the central section as well as parts passing near the outer edges. If the outer edges were adjusted properly, parts passing through the central section were not detected; if the central section was adjusted properly, spurious detections were made by the outer edges. In either case, operations were held up and could produce improperly trimmed parts.

An additional problem was that the air used for ejecting the parts became turbulent at the detector, sometime resulting in spurious detection errors.

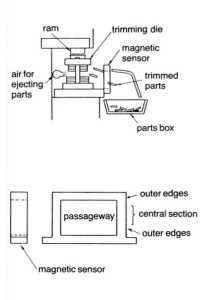

After Improvement:

The parts guides to the magnetic sensor were improved so that when small parts are processed only the bottom outer edge of the detector is used. The detector now can be adjusted to prevent spurious detection. Plastic, not sensitive to magnetism, is used in the new guide to prevent detection errors. In addition, the outlet guide has many small holes to improve the flow of air through the detector. These small holes are shaped so the parts will not cling to them.

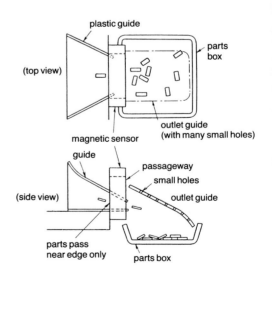

● *Example 212*

Process: Pressure-forming rivets from wire stock

Problem: Seams on finished rivets

Solution: Improve incoming materials inspections

Key Improvement: Procedure added for error detection

Prevent Error: X

Detect Error:

Shutdown:

Control: X

Alarm:

Description of Process: Rivets are pressure-formed from wire stock.

Before Improvement:

Numerous rivets had seams in them, rendering them defective and unusable. Sorting the rivets visually after pressure-forming did not solve the problem, and some defective parts were always overlooked.

wire stock   pressure-forming machine

die   punch

ingot (300 kg or more)

wire stock

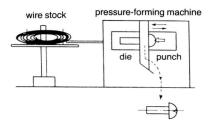

typical places where seams occurred

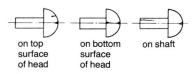

on top   on bottom   on shaft
surface   surface
of head   of head

After Improvement:

The cause of the seams was determined to be scratches in the ingots used as raw material for the wire stock. These scratches are not removed completely before the ingots are rolled and drawn, and so turn up as seams in the wire stock.

To improve the situation, the acceptance standards for the wire stock were upgraded. Defects are completely eliminated by thorough implementation of acceptance inspections, which allow no acceptance of wire stock with seams. This is a good example of *source inspection* to eliminate the causes of defects.

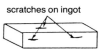

scratches on ingot

wire stock with seams completely removed

wire stock with seams remaining

● *Example 213*

Process: Assembly of fans

Problem: Backward rotating fans not detected

Solution: Change inspection method

Key Improvement: Procedure modified to detect defective parts

Prevent Error:

Detect Error:　X

Shutdown:

Control:

Alarm:　X

Description of Process: Ventilation fans are assembled, tested, and shipped. One of the tests checks that the fan rotates the correct direction.

Before Improvement:

The direction of rotation was tested after installation of the blades by checking the direction of air flow. Due to misunderstandings of the inspectors, some backwards-rotating fans were shipped to customers, and complaints were received.

nondefective item

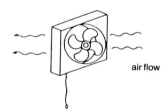

air flow

defective item

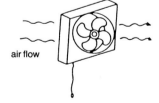

air flow

After Improvement:

Before mounting the blades a generator is placed against the fan motor shaft and the motor is operated. If the motor rotates backwards, the polarity of the generator output is wrong, and a light and a buzzer notify the inspector.

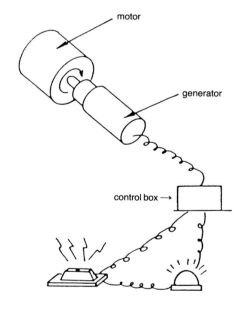

motor

generator

control box →

Wiring/Contact Errors

● *Example 214*

Process: Wiring power supply transformers

Problem: Wiring errors

Solution: Provide wiring connectors

Key Improvement: Part modified to guarantee correct positioning

Prevent Error: X

Detect Error:

Shutdown:

Control: X

Alarm:

Description of Process: In this process, power supply transformers are wired. They are extremely dangerous if they are wired incorrectly.

Before Improvement:

The colors of the wires were used to determine the correct wiring pattern of the transformers. However, mistaken wiring occurred, and worker and product safety was jeopardized.

After Improvement:

A directional three-prong connector is now used to prevent wiring errors. It is impossible to connect the wires incorrectly, and errors in wiring the transformers are completely eliminated.

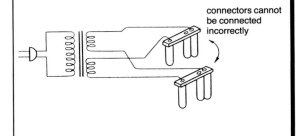

connectors cannot be connected incorrectly

● *Example 215*

Process: Wiring terminal boards

Problem: Wiring errors

Solution: One-touch wiring template

Key Improvement: Template used for assembly

Prevent Error: X

Detect Error:

Shutdown:

Control: X

Alarm:

Description of Process: Cables of many different sizes and colors are wired to a multipoint terminal board.

Before Improvement:

The workers followed a diagram mounted over the terminal board. Defects occurred because of misunderstandings, mix-ups, or oversights made when workers looked from the diagram to the wiring work.

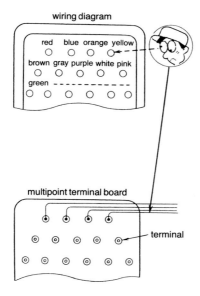

After Improvement:

A wiring template was made that slides between the rows of terminals on the board. Samples of the correct wire for each terminal are attached to the template, and the worker can tell at a glance which terminal to connect with a particular wire.

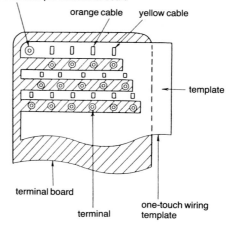

● *Example 216*

Process: Cabling control equipment

Problem: Wiring errors

Solution: One-touch wiring template

Key Improvement: Template used for assembly

Prevent Error: X

Detect Error:

Shutdown:

Control: X

Alarm:

Description of Process: A type of control equipment is produced in numerous models and the cable connections are extremely varied.

Before Improvement:

The worker consulted a diagram of the correct wiring for each model, then looked away to wire the product. Faulty wiring connections were made often as a result of oversights, misunderstandings, or faulty selection of cables.

terminal number	cable type	cable color
1	small	red
2	small	blue
3	large	green
4	large	yellow
5	small	brown

product

terminals — red blue green
1 2 3
terminal plate

After Improvement:

A set of templates was made that fit onto the terminal section of the control equipment. Samples of the actual cables to be used are mounted on the templates, and the cables are connected to the terminals in accordance with these cable samples.

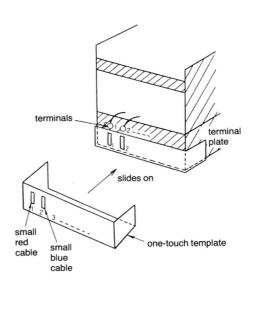

terminals — terminal plate

slides on

small red cable — small blue cable — one-touch template

● *Example 217*

Process: Shielding electrical lead terminals

Problem: Danger of short circuit in case of damage from vibration

Solution: Remove danger of short circuit

Key Improvement: Part modified to protect it from damage

Prevent Error: X

Detect Error:

Shutdown:

Control: X

Alarm:

Description of Process: The lead terminals of induction coils are insulated with a protective plastic tube.

Before Improvement:

The plastic tube rested on the metal case of the product. If the tube was damaged by vibration, there was danger that the terminals would contact the metal case and cause short circuits.

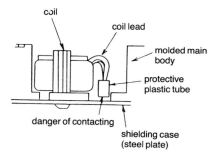

After Improvement:

The shape of the molded plastic main body was changed to provide a niche for the plastic tube. The danger of short circuits is completely eliminated. The expense for this improvement is the cost of remodeling the die for molding the main body.

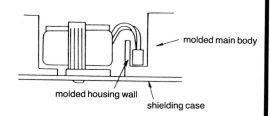

● *Example 218*

Process: Soldering connectors onto terminals   **Prevent Error:** X   **Shutdown:**

Problem: Short circuits   **Detect Error:**   **Control:** X

Solution: Improve mounting tool   **Alarm:**

Key Improvement: Tool modified to guarantee correct positioning

Description of Process: Electrical connectors are soldered onto terminals. The terminals are close to the metal shielding case of the unit, and the connectors must be bent to prevent contact with the case.

Before Improvement:

The connectors were soldered and bent manually with pliers. This resulted in considerable variation in the amount of bending, and sometimes the connector short-circuited against the case.

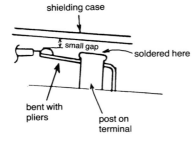

After Improvement:

A bending jig was added to the soldering iron so that the connector is bent a standard amount while being soldered to the terminal. Now anyone can solder this item correctly. The connectors no longer short-circuit against the case, and operating efficiency has increased.

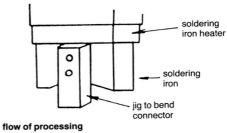

flow of processing

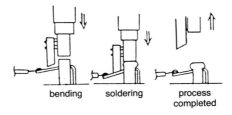

Painting Errors

● *Example 219*

Process: Electrostatic painting

Problem: Loss of high air pressure

Solution: Improve warning method

Key Improvement: Warning method improved

Prevent Error: X

Detect Error:

Shutdown:

Control:

Alarm: X

Description of Process: An operator working inside a paint booth paints fuel tanks with an electrostatic painting machine. To prevent defects it is important that the operator know if the electrostatic machine loses its high air pressure.

Before Improvement:

A buzzer sounded when pressure dropped below a certain level. However, it was so noisy in the paint booth that the operator often did not hear the buzzer and did not realize that the pressure had been lost. A warning lamp could not be used due to the fire hazard of a light bulb in the paint booth.

After Improvement:

The electric signal indicating a pressure drop now sends a mechanical visual warning to the operator in addition to the buzzer. The operator can see the signal flag when it pops out and can take prompt action to prevent defects.

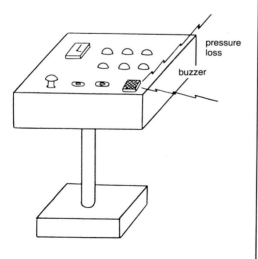

pressure loss

buzzer

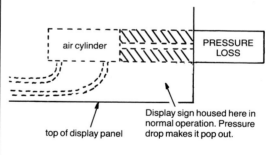

air cylinder

PRESSURE LOSS

top of display panel

Display sign housed here in normal operation. Pressure drop makes it pop out.

● *Example 220*

Process: Painting brackets

Problem: Paint deposited on inside of brackets

Solution: Improve holding rack

Key Improvement: Procedure modified to guarantee correct processing

Prevent Error: X

Detect Error:

Shutdown:

Control: X

Alarm:

Description of Process: Brackets were placed in holding racks to have their outsides spray painted.

Before Improvement:

Paint was sometimes deposited accidentally on the inside of the brackets where it should not have gone. These brackets had to be discarded.

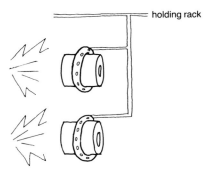

paint gets on inside

After Improvement:

A new rack was devised that sandwiches the bracket between a bottom plate and a magnetic cap to keep paint from getting on the inside.

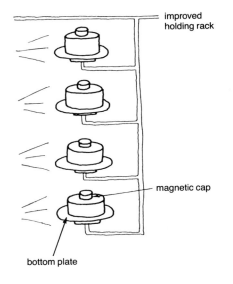

improved holding rack

magnetic cap

bottom plate

Printing Errors

● *Example 221*

Process: Printing tuner scales for car radios   **Prevent Error:** X   **Shutdown:**

Problem: Frequency numbers printed upside down   **Detect Error:**   **Control:** X

Solution: Use asymmetry of scale plate   **Alarm:**

Key Improvement: Jig modified to guarantee correct positioning

---

Description of Process: Scale plates for car radios are printed with frequency numbers.

Before Improvement:

     Sometimes the frequency numbers were printed on the scale plates upside down. This was discovered only when the scale plates were being soldered onto the escutcheons of the car radios.

After Improvement:

     A boss was mounted on the jig for printing the scale plates, using one of the soldering holes on the plate to ensure the correct orientation when printing. Upside down printing is completely eliminated.

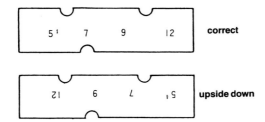

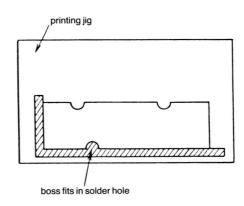

● *Example 222*

Process: Printing

Problem: Marks printed upside down or out of position

Solution: Guide pins on jig use notches on part

Key Improvement: Jig modified to guarantee correct positioning

Prevent Error: X

Detect Error:

Shutdown:

Control: X

Alarm:

Description of Process: Parts are printed with various numbers and marks.

Before Improvement:

It was possible to put the part in the printing jig in several different ways, only one of which was correct. As a result, marks were printed upside down or out of position.

After Improvement:

Two guide pins were added to the printing jig. Marks printed upside down or out of position are completely eliminated.

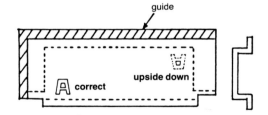

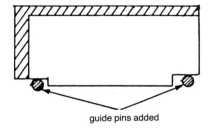

guide pins added

Misalignment

● *Example 223*

Process: Topstitching sash borders

Problem: Uneven stitching

Solution: Stitching lines in interfacing used as guide

Key Improvement: Procedure modified to guarantee correct processing

Prevent Error: X

Detect Error:

Shutdown:

Control: X

Alarm:

Description of Process: Sash borders were topstitched 1.0 cm from the edges, using a gage next to the sewing machine needle as a guide.

Before Improvement:

There were frequently variations in the distance between the lines of stitching, and obtaining the proper width was difficult.

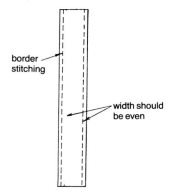

border stitching

width should be even

After Improvement:

Parallel lines were marked on a sash-shaped piece of nonwoven interfacing affixed to the back of the sash, using unthreaded needles on a converted sewing machine. The operator follows these lines when doing the topstitching, resulting in perfectly parallel stitching lines.

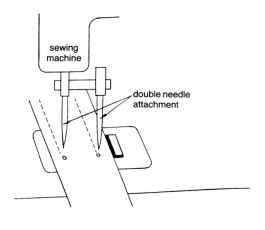

sewing machine

double needle attachment

● *Example 224*

Process: Sewing shirt collars

Problem: Inspecting for uneven stitching

Solution: Use gage instead of ruler

Key Improvement: Gage used for inspection

Prevent Error:

Detect Error: X

Shutdown:

Control: X

Alarm:

Description of Process: Shirt collars are sewn semiautomatically from (1) to (2) in the drawing. It is most important that the line from (3) to (4) is sewn 2.8 cm from the border.

Before Improvement:

Inspections were made with a ruler after sewing, but it was easy to misread the scale and pass on defective items.

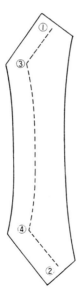

After Improvement:

A gage was developed so it is easy to check whether the 2.8 cm line has been followed.

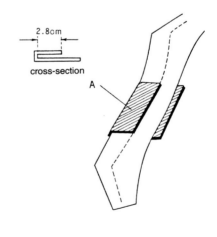

Set-Up Errors

● *Example 225*

Process: Transfer press setup

Problem: Feed bar fingers inserted in wrong slots

Solution: Fingers made noninterchangeable

Key Improvement: Tool modified to guarantee correct positioning

Prevent Error: X

Detect Error:

Shutdown:

Control: X

Alarm:

Description of Process: Part of the process of setting up the transfer press is to replace the twenty-four left and right feed bar fingers in a particular pattern.

Before Improvement:

The sockets in the feed bar all had the same dimensions, and the fingers could be mounted in the wrong order.

After Improvement:

Notches were made in the mounting end of the left fingers, and poka-yoke pins were mounted in the corresponding sockets of the feed bar so that right fingers could not be mounted there. It is now impossible to mount the fingers in the wrong position on the feed bar.

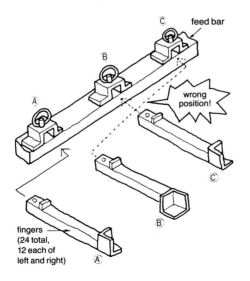

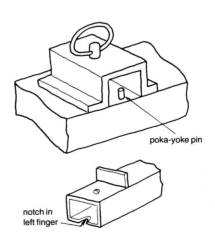

● *Example 226*

Process: Press setup

Problem: Cable snapped during die changeover

Solution: Prevent die movement while cable is attached

Key Improvement: Tool modified to protect it from damage

Prevent Error: X

Detect Error:

Shutdown:

Control: X

Alarm:

Description of Process: When changing the setup on a large press, the old die moves out of the press and the new die moves in from the other side. This transport mechanism is actuated by a switch. Each die is also equipped with circuitry to detect the presence of the workpiece during processing, which is connected to the press controls by a cable. The cable must be disconnected before the dies are moved.

Before Improvement:

When changing dies the worker was to make a visual check of the cable. The standard procedure had instructions for this, but sometimes the cable was not removed before the die was moved. This snapped the cable or pulled and damaged the connecting terminals.

After Improvement:

Two unused terminals in the terminal box on the die were jumpered. The switch operating the die transport mechanism is interlocked with this circuit so that the transport switch does not operate while the cable is connected.

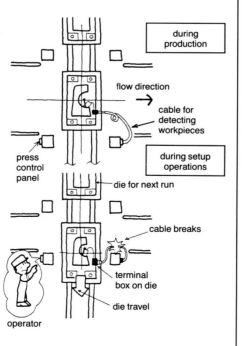

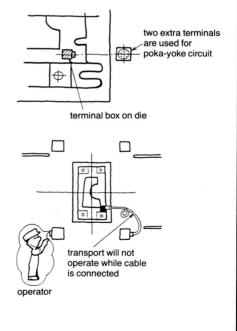

Packing/Wrapping Errors

● *Example 227*

Process: Automatic wrapping

Problem: Torn wrapping paper

Solution: Moisten paper

Key Improvement: Tool modified to guarantee correct processing

Prevent Error: X

Detect Error:

Shutdown:

Control: X

Alarm:

Description of Process: Product units are fed through an automatic machine that folds a paper wrapper around each one.

Before Improvement:

The corners were sometimes torn during folding, as shown in the drawing, resulting in faulty wrapping. A worker was specially assigned to check the external appearance of each package and rewrap when necessary.

After Improvement:

An investigation into the characteristics of the paper and what conditions make it least susceptible to tearing revealed that the paper is more flexible when slightly damp. A nozzle is used to spray a small burst of steam immediately before folding to give a suitable amount of moisture. This completely eliminates tearing, and a worker no longer has to check the wrapping.

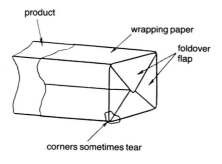

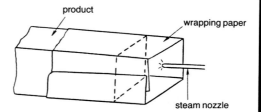

● *Example 228*

Process: Packing delivery boxes

Problem: Omission of accessories

Solution: Count accessories packed

Key Improvement: Selection of parts automated

Prevent Error: X

Detect Error:

Shutdown:

Control: X

Alarm:

Description of Process: Two workers are assigned to (1) assemble boxes, (2) clean and pack the main units, and (3) pack the six different accessories (such as instruction manuals and cords).

Before Improvement:

The workers sometimes forgot to pack some of the accessories when they were working in a hurry, as in the case when a large number of main units had just completed inspection.

After Improvement:

A new accessory supply rack was designed, with photoelectric switches mounted on the fronts of the boxes housing the different accessories. A switch turns on each time the light is interrupted by the worker taking out an accessory. A pop-up stopper keeps the box containing the main unit from traveling further along the conveyor until all six switches have turned on. When the box is allowed to pass, it trips a limit switch that resets the photoelectric switches to their starting state.

accessories

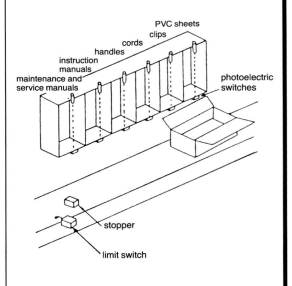

PVC sheets
clips
cords
handles
instruction
manuals
maintenance and
service manuals
photoelectric
switches
stopper
limit switch

Mismatched Jigs and Dies

● *Example 229*

Process: Press setup

Problem: Mismatched top and bottom jig

Solution: Use pins to prevent setup with mismatched jigs

Key Improvement: Jig modified to guarantee correct positioning

Prevent Error: X

Detect Error:

Shutdown:

Control: X

Alarm:

Description of Process: For some models manufactured, both the upper and lower jigs of the press are changed during setup.

Before Improvement:

The only check on the setup operations was the operator. On rare occasions the operator set the wrong upper jig in place and ran the press, resulting in defects.

correct

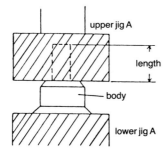

incorrect

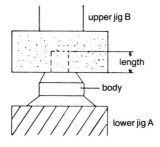

After Improvement:

Because the upper and lower jigs are always used together as a set, different pins and guides were installed on each set. If the incorrect upper jig is used, the pin on the lower jig prevents the press from closing.

correct

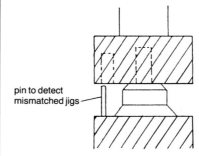

wrong jig won't fit

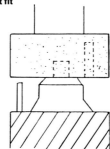

● *Example 230*

Process: Setting up press dies

Prevent Error: X

Shutdown:

Problem: Die breakage and defective press forming

Detect Error:

Control: X

Solution: Vary guide pins to prevent closing in incorrect position

Alarm:

Key Improvement: Tool modified to protect it from damage

Description of Process: Press dies are used to form small components.

Before Improvement:

Since the guide pins for fitting the upper and lower dies together had the same diameter, it was possible to mount the upper die reversed 180 degrees from its correct position. Errors when assembling the dies caused defective pressing or breakage of the dies.

After Improvement:

The left and right guide pins for fitting the dies together were given different diameters so the dies cannot be closed in the wrong position.

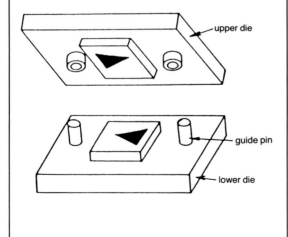

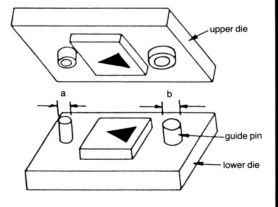

Rinsing Errors

● *Example 231*

Process: Preliminary rinsing of parts   **Prevent Error:** X   **Shutdown:**

Problem: Rinsing omitted or wrong parts rinsed   **Detect Error:**   **Control:** X

Solution: Improved limit switch   **Alarm:**

Key Improvement: Tool modified to guarantee correct processing

Description of Process: Machined parts receive a preliminary rinsing, except for those parts coated with preservatives. The parts move to the rinsing area in baskets, some of which have no-rinse detection terminals mounted on them to be detected by a limit switch before the rinse.

Before Improvement:

Baskets positioned toward the left side of the conveyor did not trip the limit switch, even if they had no-rinse terminals, and were rinsed. On the other hand, baskets positioned on the right side sometimes tripped the no-rinse limit switch even though they did not have no-rinse terminals and should have been rinsed.

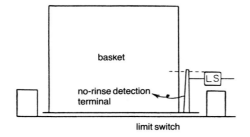

limit switch

After Improvement:

The limit switch was modified so that it detects a no-rinse terminal even when the basket is toward the left side of the conveyor. The limit switch was also mounted on a spring hinge so that only a no-rinse terminal trips it if a basket comes down the right side of the conveyor. If a basket without such a terminal comes down the right side, the basket bends over the entire switch mechanism instead of tripping it, and the parts are rinsed as they should be.

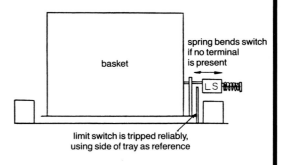

limit switch is tripped reliably, using side of tray as reference

● *Example 232*

Process: Cleaning storage tanks

Problem: Cleaning wrong tanks

Solution: Add noninterchangeable keys to cleaning process control circuit

Key Improvement: Procedure modified to guarantee correct processing

Prevent Error: X

Detect Error:

Shutdown:

Control: X

Alarm:

Description of Process: Empty tanks are cleaned in place. A worker uses a control board to switch on the circuit for the tank to be cleaned.

Before Improvement:

The operator visually determined which tank was to be cleaned, then made the connection on the control board. Sometimes the connection was inadvertently made to the circuit for the wrong tank. The nonempty tank would be filled with water by mistake, ruining the contents.

After Improvement:

Each connection on the control board is protected by a key switch. Each tank has its own key, marked with a distinctive shape and stored in a correspondingly shaped frame on the tank. The key will fit only its switch on the control board and it cannot be put back on the wrong tank. To initiate the cleaning-in-place process, the worker takes the key from the tank to be cleaned and inserts it in the proper keyhole on the board. It is now impossible to clean the wrong tank.

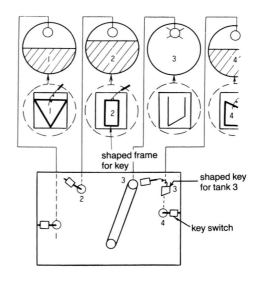

Miscellaneous Problems

● *Example 233*

Process: Cassette deck sliding control knobs   **Prevent Error:** X   **Shutdown:**

Problem: Dust created by friction of metal knob caps   **Detect Error:**   **Control:**   X
against plastic body

Solution: Change aluminum/plastic contact to plastic/plastic   **Alarm:**

Key Improvement: Part modified to protect it from damage

Description of Process: The cassette deck was designed with aluminum caps on the control knobs.

Before Improvement:

    Fine dust was created when the aluminum knob cap moved against the molded plastic guide. Applying grease was an unsatisfactory solution because it was black and took time to apply carefully.

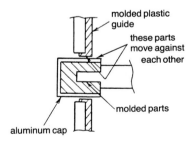

After Improvement:

    The shapes of the knob and guide were changed so that only plastic parts move against each other. The dust is eliminated and the greasing operation is not required.

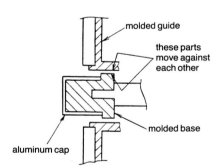

● *Example 234*

Process: Greasing ground fixture on cassette decks   **Prevent Error:** X   **Shutdown:**

Problem: Grease on pulley belt   **Detect Error:**   **Control:** X

Solution: Install stopper on grease brush so pulley belt can't be greased   **Alarm:**

Key Improvement: Tool modified to guarantee correct processing

Description of Process: A ground fixture on a cassette deck mechanism is greased with white grease, applied with a brush. However, if grease accidentally gets on the nearby pulley belt, the auto-stop mechanism will not work.

Before Improvement:

Despite the vigilance of skilled workers, grease sometimes got on the pulley belt, causing defects.

After Improvement:

The brush was outfitted with a stopper so the brush cannot reach all the way to the belt. Grease no longer gets on the belt, and auto-stop failures are completely eliminated. The addition of the stopper makes it possible for experienced workers and novices to do the work equally well.

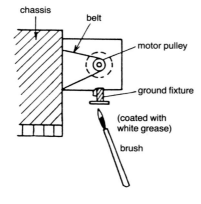

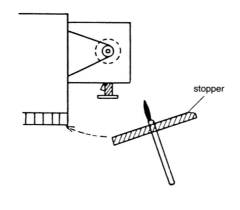

● *Example 235*

Process: Casting

Problem: Unreliable pressure gauges

Solution: Install redundant pressure gauges for comparison

Key Improvement: Tool modified to make additional test

Prevent Error:

Detect Error: X

Shutdown:

Control: X

Alarm:

Description of Process: When casting products with a large casting machine, undesired changes in machine conditions can result in blowholes and other defects. Pressure gauges are installed at key locations to monitor the casting process and the state of the machine.

Before Improvement:

One pressure gauge was installed at each measuring site, but if a gauge was reading a non-standard condition, it was difficult to determine whether it was the process or the gauge at fault.

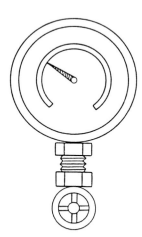

After Improvement:

Two pressure gauges are installed on the same outlet at each measuring site. The operator can quickly determine the reliability of the readings on the gauges by comparing them.

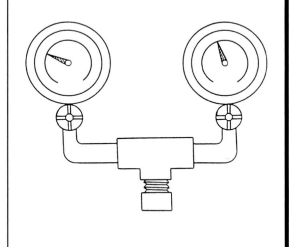

● *Example 236*

Process: Welding

Problem: Welding omitted

Solution: Mechanically sort unprocessed parts

Key Improvement: Chute modified to sort out defective parts

Prevent Error:

Detect Error: X

Shutdown:

Control: X

Alarm:

Description of Process: Shafts are welded to bushings in an automatic welding machine. Sometimes the welding machine does not weld the parts, for one reason or another. The unwelded bushings must be separated from the welded parts before assembly.

Before Improvement:

One worker was specially assigned to the work of sorting out the unwelded bushings. Even so, they sometimes got by and usually led to faulty assembly. Complaints were received from the users.

After Improvement:

Using the fact that the unwelded bushing is missing the shaft, a mechanical sorter was developed to remove the faulty parts from the transport line.

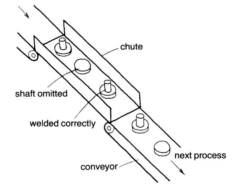

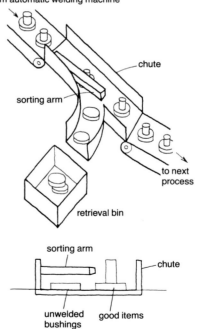

● *Example 237*

Process: Chemically treating plastic film   **Prevent Error:** X   **Shutdown:** X

Problem: Downtime to reload after film breakage   **Detect Error:**   **Control:**

Solution: Detect tears early enough to avoid breakage in machine   **Alarm:**

Key Improvement: Process modified to protect part from damage

Description of Process: Plastic film is subjected to a continuous chemical process. The process takes place in a high-temperature chemical bath. To repair film that breaks inside the process, it is necessary to wait for the machinery to cool before opening the chemical bath. Often cuts and tears occur at the feed rollers just before the film enters the machine. If the cuts or tears enter the machine, the film is likely to break and bring processing to a halt while the machine is reloaded.

Before Improvement:

Whenever cuts or tears occurred, the machine had to be stopped and reloaded, causing large losses of processing time.

After Improvement:

Three photoelectric sensors are installed in front of the feed rollers to detect cuts or tears. When a cut or tear is detected, the film feed and the processing machine both stop. The film is repaired before it enters the machine, so breaks rarely occur inside the machine. Downtime due to reloading the machine has been reduced to a minimum.

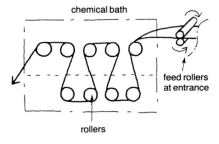

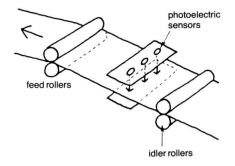

● *Example 238*

Process: Various

Problem: Various

Solution: Use of mirrors for improvement

Key Improvement: Various

Prevent Error: X

Detect Error: X

Shutdown:

Control: X

Alarm: X

Description of Process: A variety of processes and situations around the plant were improved by the use of different kinds of mirrors.

Before Improvement:

Mirrors had been given little importance until one worker proposed some improvements using hand mirrors. This led to a broader investigation to expand the use of mirrors in the plant.

Checking the bottom surface of an upper die.

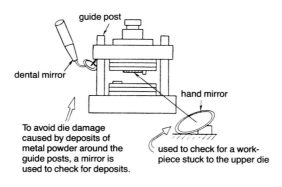

To avoid die damage caused by deposits of metal powder around the guide posts, a mirror is used to check for deposits.

used to check for a work-piece stuck to the upper die

Mirrors located on passageways throughout the plant not only allow pedestrians and vehicles to avoid collisions, but also prevent pedestrians from bumping into each other, particularly when they are carrying materials from one area to another.

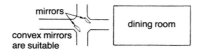

convex mirrors are suitable

After Improvement:

Examples of using mirrors for improvement:

Preventing errors when an increased number of automatic machines are assigned to one worker.

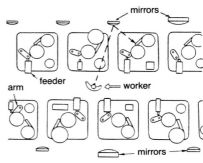

convex mirrors are suitable

Preventing errors in operations caused by worn or broken tips of staking punches.

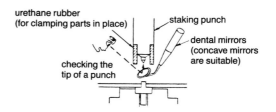

urethane rubber (for clamping parts in place)

staking punch

dental mirrors (concave mirrors are suitable)

checking the tip of a punch

● *Example 239*

Process: Removing a few products a day from the production line

Problem: Auxiliary lifting jig not removed

Solution: Make jig itself remind workers it needs to be removed

Key Improvement: Jig modified to guarantee correct processing

Prevent Error: X

Detect Error:

Shutdown:

Control:

Alarm: X

Description of Process: A few times a day there is an operation where workers use a hand lifter to take products off the production line. For these special products an auxiliary jig is put on the hand lifter. After the products have been taken off the line, the auxiliary jig has to be removed before the product goes to the next process.

Before Improvement:

The auxiliary jigs were mounted in a position where they were hard to see, and their color was the same as the surrounding objects. Because the operation took place only a few times a day, the worker sometimes forgot to remove the auxiliary jigs after the products had been taken off the production line and the jigs moved on to the subsequent processes. To solve this problem the auxiliary jigs were painted red to make them more noticeable, but there were still failures to remove the jigs.

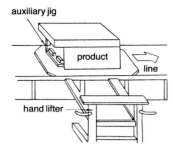

After Improvement:

The process of mounting the auxiliary jig, taking the products off the line, and removing the auxiliary jig takes a very short time. Therefore a microswitch, battery, and buzzer were mounted on the auxiliary jig. The buzzer sounds as soon as the jig is set in place, and there is no time for the worker to get used to the sound and ignore it. Thanks to this improvement, the workers no longer forget to remove the auxiliary jigs.

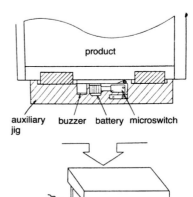

● *Example 240*

Process: Moving goods with an overhead crane   **Prevent Error:** X   **Shutdown:**

Problem: Dangerous swinging loads   **Detect Error:**   **Control:** X

Solution: Stop crane gradually at ends of travel   **Alarm:**

Key Improvement: Tool modified to protect it from damage

Description of Process: A suspended overhead crane is used to transport goods throughout a section of the factory.

Before Improvement:

Mechanical stoppers are mounted at the ends of the rails on which the crane travels. Sometimes when the crane was traveling at a fast speed or had traveled only a short distance it would strike against the stoppers rather violently. This caused the loads to swing, resulting in a dangerous situation.

After Improvement:

A limit switch was mounted on the crane and contacting fixtures were mounted on the traveling rails just before the stoppers. When the limit switch on the crane hits the contacting fixtures, the crane motor is stopped, and the crane continues to move only under inertial force. The crane no longer stops suddenly after moving at high speed. This mitigates shocks and prevents swinging of loads without any vigilance on the part of the crane operator.

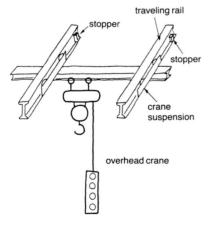

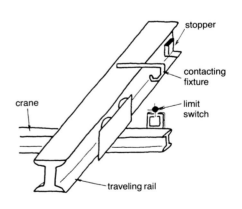

Poka-yoke Improvement Form

We hope you — individuals as well as study groups — will actively discuss, use, copy, adapt, multiply, and improve on the ideas compiled here. On the next page is a blank improvement form you can photocopy. Use it to sketch out and record your own ideas.

● *Example*

Process: **Prevent Error:**   **Shutdown:**

Problem: **Detect Error:**   **Control:**

Solution: **Alarm:**

Key Improvement:

Description of Process:

Before Improvement:	**After Improvement:**

Indexes

References are to example numbers.

**Index of Operations,
Processes, and Problems**

References are to example numbers.

References are to example numbers.

Index of Devices and Methods

References are to example numbers.

References are to example numbers.

Index of Parts and Products

References are to example numbers.

References are to example numbers.

OTHER BOOKS ON QUALITY

Productivity Press publishes and distributes materials on continuous improvement in productivity, quality, customer service, and the creative involvement of all employees. Many of our products are direct source materials from Japan that have been translated into English for the first time and are available exclusively from Productivity. Supplemental products and services include newsletters, conferences, seminars, in-house training and consulting, audio-visual training programs, and industrial study missions. Call 1-800-274-9911 for our free book catalog.

Quality Function Deployment
Integrating Customer Requirements into Product Design
Yoji Akao (ed.)

More and more, companies are using quality function deployment, or QFD, to identify their customers' requirements, translate them into quantified quality characteristics and then build them into their products and services. This casebook introduces the concept of quality deployment as it has been applied in a variety of industries in Japan. The materials include numerous case studies illustrating QFD applications. Written by the creator of QFD, this book provides direct source material on Quality Function Deployment, one of the essential tools for world class manufacturing. It is a design approach based on the idea that quality is determined by the customer. Through methodology and case studies the book offers insight into how Japanese companies identify customer requirements and describes how to translate customer requirements into qualified quality characteristics, and how to build them into products and services.
ISBN 0-915299-41-0 / 400 pages / $ 75.00 / Order code QFD-BK

Handbook of Quality Tools
The Japanese Approach
Tetsuichi Asaka and Kazuo Ozeki (eds.)

The Japanese have stunned the world by their ability to produce top quality products at competitive prices. This comprehensive teaching manual, which includes the 7 traditional and 5 newer QC tools, explains each tool, why it's useful, and how to construct and use it. Information is presented in easy-to-grasp language, with step-by-step instructions, illustrations, and examples of each tool. A perfect training aid, as well as a hands-on reference book, for supervisors, foremen, and/or team leaders. Here's the best resource on the myriad Japanese quality tools changing the face of world manufacturing today. Accessible to everyone in your organization, dealing with both management and shop floor how-to's, you'll find it an indispensable tool in your quest for quality.
ISBN 0-915299-45-3 / 336 pages / $59.95 / Order code HQT-BK

Productivity Press, Inc., Dept. BK, P.O. Box 3007, Cambridge, MA 02140 1-800-274-9911

TQC Solutions
The 14-Step Process
JUSE Problem Solving Research Group (ed.)
Foreword by Dr. H. James Harrington

Here's a clear-cut, thoroughly explained process for putting the tools of quality control to work in your company. With a strong emphasis on the use of quality control in problem solving, this book was originally written as a handbook for the Union of Japanese Scientists and Engineers' (JUSE) renowned Quality Control seminar. Filled with practical, highly useful information, it shows you not only *how* to use the 7 QC tools, the 7 "new" QC tools, and basic statistical tools, but also suggests *when* to use them. The use of charts and matrices in problem solving is carefully examined and illustrated with examples of various problems and their solutions.
ISBN 0-915299-79-8 / 448 pages, 2 volumes / $120.00 / Order TQCS-BK

Management for Quality Improvement
The 7 New QC Tools

Shigeru Mizuno (ed.)

Building on the traditional seven QC tools, these new tools were developed specifically for managers. They help in planning, troubleshooting, and communicating with maximum effectiveness at every stage of a quality improvement program. Just recently made available in the U.S., they are certain to advance quality improvement efforts for anyone involved in project management, quality assurance, MIS, or TQC.
ISBN 0-915299-29-1 / 324 pages / $59.95 / Order code 7QC-BK

Achieving Total Quality Management
A Program for Action

Michel Perigord

This is an outstanding book on total quality management (TQM) a compact guide to the concepts, methods, and techniques involved in achieving total quality. It shows you how to make TQM a company-wide strategy, not just in technical areas, but in marketing and administration as well. Written in an accessible, instructive style by a top European quality expert, it is methodical, logical, and thorough. An historical outline anddiscussion of the quality-price relationship, is followed by an investigation of the five quality imperatives (conformity, prevention, excellence, measurement, and responsibility). Major methods and tools for total quality are spelled out and implementation strategies are reviewed.
ISBN 0-915299-60-7 / 384 pages / $45.00 / Order Code ACHTQM-BK

Audio Visual Training Aid

The Poka-Yoke System Shigeo Shingo, translated by Andrew P. Dillon Shingo shows how to implement Zero Quality Control (ZQC) on the production line with a combination of source inspection and mistake-proofing devices in this two-part program. Part I explains the theory and concepts and Part II shows practical applications. Package includes facilitator's guides with worksheets, and is available in either slide or video format (please specify when ordering). Each part is approximately 25 minutes long.
235 Slides / ISBN 0-915299-13-5 / $749.00 / Order code S6-BK
2 Videos / ISBN 0-915299-28-3 / $749.00 / Order code V6-BK

Productivity Press, Inc., Dept. BK, P.O. Box 3007, Cambridge, MA 02140 1-800-274-9911

COMPLETE LIST OF TITLES FROM PRODUCTIVITY PRESS

Akao, Yoji (ed.). **Quality Function Deployment: Integrating Customer Requirements into Product Design**
ISBN 0-915299-41-0 / 1990 / 387 pages / $ 75.00 / order code QFD

Akiyama, Kaneo. **Function Analysis: Systematic Improvement of Quality and Performance**
ISBN 0-915299-81-X / 1991 / 288 pages / $59.95 / order code FA

Asaka, Tetsuichi and Kazuo Ozeki (eds.). **Handbook of Quality Tools: The Japanese Approach**
ISBN 0-915299-45-3 / 1990 / 336 pages / $59.95 / order code HQT

Belohlav, James A. **Championship Management: An Action Model for High Performance**
ISBN 0-915299-76-3 / 1990 / 265 pages / $29.95 / order code CHAMPS

Birkholz, Charles and Jim Villella. **The Battle to Stay Competitive: Changing the Traditional Workplace**
ISBN 0-915-299-96-8 / 1991 / 110 pages / $9.95 /order code BATTLE

Christopher, William F. **Productivity Measurement Handbook**
ISBN 0-915299-05-4 / 1985 / 680 pages / $137.95 / order code PMH

D'Egidio, Franco. **The Service Era: Leadership in a Global Environment**
ISBN 0-915299-68-2 / 1990 / 165 pages / $29.95 / order code SERA

Ford, Henry. **Today and Tomorrow**
ISBN 0-915299-36-4 / 1988 / 286 pages / $24.95 / order code FORD

Fukuda, Ryuji. **CEDAC: A Tool for Continuous Systematic Improvement**
ISBN 0-915299-26-7 / 1990 / 144 pages / $49.95 / order code CEDAC

Fukuda, Ryuji. **Managerial Engineering: Techniques for Improving Quality and Productivity in the Workplace** (rev.)
ISBN 0-915299-09-7 / 1986 / 208 pages / $39.95 / order code ME

Gotoh, Fumio. **Equipment Planning for TPM: Maintenance Prevention Design**
ISBN 0-915299-77-1 / 1991 / 320 pages / $75.00 / order code ETPM

Grief, Michel. **The Visual Factory: Building Participation Through Shared Information**
ISBN 0-915299-67-4 / 1991 / 320 pages / $49.95 / order code VFAC

Hatakeyama, Yoshio. **Manager Revolution! A Guide to Survival in Today's Changing Workplace**
ISBN 0-915299-10-0 / 1986 / 208 pages / $24.95 / order code MREV

Hirano, Hiroyuki. **JIT Factory Revolution: A Pictorial Guide to Factory Design of the Future**
ISBN 0-915299-44-5 / 1989 / 227 pages / $49.95 / order code JITFAC

Hirano, Hiroyuki. **JIT Implementation Manual: The Complete Guide to Just-In-Time Manufacturing**
ISBN 0-915299-66-6 / 1990 / 1006 pages / $2500.00 / order code HIRANO

Horovitz, Jacques. **Winning Ways: Achieving Zero-Defect Service**
ISBN 0-915299-78-X / 1990 / 165 pages / $24.95 / order code WWAYS

Ishiwata, Junichi. **I.E. for the Shop Floor 1: Productivity Through Process Analysis**
ISBN 0-915299-82-8 / 1991 / 208 pages / $39.95 / order code SHOPF1

Japan Human Relations Association (ed.). **The Idea Book: Improvement Through TEI (Total Employee Involvement)**
ISBN 0-915299-22-4 / 1988 / 232 pages / $49.95 / order code IDEA

Productivity Press, Inc., Dept. BK, P.O. Box 3007, Cambridge, MA 02140 1-800-274-9911

Japan Human Relations Association (ed.). **The Service Industry Idea Book: Employee Involvement in Retail and Office Improvement**
ISBN 0-915299-65-8 / 1991 / 294 pages / $49.95 / order code SIDEA

Japan Management Association (ed.). **Kanban and Just-In-Time at Toyota: Management Begins at the Workplace** (rev.), Translated by David J. Lu
ISBN 0-915299-48-8 / 1989 / 224 pages / $36.50 / order code KAN

Japan Management Association and Constance E. Dyer. **The Canon Production System: Creative Involvement of the Total Workforce**
ISBN 0-915299-06-2 / 1987 / 251 pages / $36.95 / order code CAN

Jones, Karen (ed.). **The Best of TEI: Current Perspectives on Total Employee Involvement**
ISBN 0-915299-63-1 / 1989 / 502 pages / $175.00 / order code TEI

JUSE. **TQC Solutions: The 14-Step Process**
ISBN 0-915299-79-8 / 1991 / 416 pages / 2 volumes / $120.00 / order code TQCS

Kanatsu, Takashi. **TQC for Accounting: A New Role in Companywide Improvement**
ISBN 0-915299-73-9 / 1991 / 244 pages / $45.00 / order code TQCA

Karatsu, Hajime. **Tough Words For American Industry**
ISBN 0-915299-25-9 / 1988 / 178 pages / $24.95 / order code TOUGH

Karatsu, Hajime. **TQC Wisdom of Japan: Managing for Total Quality Control**, Translated by David J. Lu
ISBN 0-915299-18-6 / 1988 / 136 pages / $34.95 / order code WISD

Kato, Kenichiro. **I.E. for the Shop FLoor 2: Productivity Through Motion Study**
ISBN 1-56327-000-5 / 1991 / 224 pages / $39.95 / order code SHOPF2

Kaydos, Will. **Measuring, Managing, and Maximizing Performance**
ISBN 0-915299-98-4 / 1991 / 304 pages / $34.95 / order code MMMP

Kobayashi, Iwao. **20 Keys to Workplace Improvement**
ISBN 0-915299-61-5 / 1990 / 264 pages / $34.95 / order code 20KEYS

Lu, David J. **Inside Corporate Japan: The Art of Fumble-Free Management**
ISBN 0-915299-16-X / 1987 / 278 pages / $24.95 / order code ICJ

Maskell, Brain H. **Performance Measurement for World Class Manufacturing: A Model for American Companies**
ISBN 0-915299-99-2 / 1991 / 448 pages / $49.95 / order code PERFM

Merli, Giorgio. **Total Manufacturing Management: Production Organization for the 1990s**
ISBN 0-915299-58-5 / 1990 / 304 pages / $39.95 / order code TMM

Mizuno, Shigeru (ed.). **Management for Quality Improvement: The 7 New QC Tools**
ISBN 0-915299-29-1 / 1988 / 324 pages / $59.95 / order code 7QC

Monden, Yasuhiro and Michiharu Sakurai (eds.). **Japanese Management Accounting: A World Class Approach to Profit Management**
ISBN 0-915299-50-X / 1990 / 568 pages / $59.95 / order code JMACT

Nachi-Fujikoshi (ed.). **Training for TPM: A Manufacturing Success Story**
ISBN 0-915299-34-8 / 1990 / 272 pages / $59.95 / order code CTPM

Nakajima, Seiichi. **Introduction to TPM: Total Productive Maintenance**
ISBN 0-915299-23-2 / 1988 / 149 pages / $39.95 / order code ITPM

Nakajima, Seiichi. **TPM Development Program: Implementing Total Productive Maintenance**
ISBN 0-915299-37-2 / 1989 / 428 pages / $85.00 / order code DTPM

Productivity Press, Inc., Dept. BK, P.O. Box 3007, Cambridge, MA 02140 1-800-274-9911